Halloween

I want to see Halloween….. Halloween

Halloween, the curse of Michael Myers! I love Halloween movies,
I love the music – the music is so cool, it just makes me crazy.
The music is hypnotic, it makes me think of killing, which scares
me. I think I could be such a horrible person, I really could, I have
that insaneness about me - I can snap at any time if I get really
angry. I've always loved horror films, novels, and whatnot. I love
that intense adrenaline rush.

I want Billy back! I need someone to be comfortable with. I need
someone. I am helpless

Monday 12/25/95
Well today is Christmas, spent most of the day at Kelly's house,
got a really cool sweater (and this diary – added in a page I wrote
earlier in the year above)! Rick hasn't called me yet, he said that
family and friends were the most important things on Christmas, so
I guess I'm not important. Saw Billy at the basket ball game on
Friday - brought back memories. Kelly's friend Tara called him
over, we talked for a while and it was nice. Then he called me on
Saturday, I was amazed. I called him back but he wasn't home. It
was Christmas eve day and he was shopping. Being with him
again would be so nice. He really did care about me, all he wanted
to do was protect me. Well if Rick doesn't do something soon and
Billy does who knows what will happen. Boy does Billy have a
nice body - so tall and strong (heart).

Tuesday 12/26/95
My extended family came over today and my younger cousin is
turning into a real snob and the whole time they were here I keep
thinking of what I could be doing if they weren't here! Tomorrow

Kelly and I are going shopping and then to the holiday tournament - where I hope to see Billy or even Rick, neither has called me. I feel so insignificant. It's amazing how a guy can make you feel, like they have some special power or something!

Wednesday 12/27/95
I called Rick again today, turns out that he never got my message in the 1st place, we talked for a while - he's really sweet. He said he would call me on Friday (heart). Went to the holiday tournament w/Kelly - Rick was there during the 4th quarter he came over and sat w/ us. He didn't mention anything about my present or card. He asked me if I called him and I did, but of course he didn't bother to call me back. He said I MIGHT be able to spend new year's eve w/ him and Dan, but he doesn't seem to excited about the idea. He confuses me so much, I can never understand him. After the game I threw a snowball at him - socked him right in the butt! Then he chased after me and shoved a snowball down the back of my shirt. We followed them (him + Matt S.) in the car for a little, but then we were bored. I have a horrible cold and am miserable. But to top it off when I came home Robin, my mother, started up on her thing how I do drugs and all - stupid BITCH! I don't need her shit!! I have enough things to worry about like college, school, guys! To her she is always right and won't listen to anyone. If only she knew that 99% of the time she's <u>wrong</u>!

Thursday 12/28/95
Didn't really do much today. Went over to Kelly's at around eight we talked for about four hours about guys, like Billy and his big body parts and how Rick acts like a fag - with the way he walks and stuff. Billy is going to call me tomorrow!! I think I like him. This time I'll do things right. We can go to basketball games and to the movies and ice skating. We can just hang out and be buddies first, then lovers (heart).

Friday 12/29/95

Tonight I was supposed to go ice skating but Joanna broke her collarbone last night skiing, so that didn't happen. I waited for Billy to call me all day but he didn't so then I called him at 7:30. He said that he was going to the mall and asked me to meet him there, but then, because I'm sick I couldn't go, DAMN! I really wanted to see him so then I went over to Kelly's, her parents were having a party and Tony was there. He was all over me the whole night - I think he was horny. I kept thinking how nice it would have been to be with Billy or even if Billy came over to Kelly's house. I hope he doesn't think I didn't go meet him at the mall because I didn't want to, because I really did want to! Ooh, called Rick, Dan doesn't want me to spend new years with them! Rick's out for good – Billy's in!

Saturday 12/30/95

Went to the King of Prussia Mall with Kelly + her family, came home found out that grandparents were going out to dinner - Robin at Zerns, so I called Billy - picked him up at 6:30, came over for about 2 hours, awkward at first, but then things warmed up. He is so strong - can toss me around like a feather - love his body, so tempting. He kissed me on the couch in the family room! I love the feeling of him between my legs and wrapped around me! (heart)

Wednesday 1/3/96

Billy, I don't know what to do about him. He never called me, I called him today - he wasn't very thrilled. I feel so sick. He is the first thing I think of in the morning and the last thing I think of at night. I feel so pathetic that he has ditched me before. Why did he have to call me? I was so perfectly content with talking to him at the B-ball game. He had to go and start everything all over again!

Friday 1/5/96

Well I knew - Billy is an immature coward. "I don't know" is his favorite phrase. I had to beat it out of him that he doesn't like me though he has the nerve to say that he still wants to talk to me! Rick was at the B-ball game tonight, with family? He was all upset because I parked in his spot. We are so much alike - no wonder we can't get along.

Saturday 1/6/96

Went to see "Waiting to Exhale" with Kelly, really liked the movie, inspired me to be more confident and in control. Went to Taco Bell afterwards - meet a Knoll School (boarding school for boys only) guy Jeremy (great timing) said there's a Knoll dance Jan 13, that's where I'll be next Saturday - hope he finds me, he looked really cute + rich (Donald Trump Jr. goes to Knoll!). Also when I got home found out two guys had come to the door looking for me. Found out that it was James and Joe and that Lana was waiting in her car (Saab). Lana told me that it was James's idea to go to my door; he thought it would be cool to have me come smoke a bowl with them? I keep thinking that I should be real excited and all, but I'm not. Lana likes to play mind games, she probably got James to do that so that I would think that he liked me but he won't and then Lana will think it was funny that I get all worked up about it but I won't so screw her! Though I do like James, he's HOT

Saturday 1/13/96

Had a week off of school because of the snow. There was supposed to be a Knoll dance tonight but it was canceled. So me and Lana were going to hang out with Chris + James. We went to his house to pick him up but Betsy and Denise were there so we all stayed in his garage. They all were talking about me and how James supposedly wants me - Ya right They were all smoking up and chanted my name to join in - but of course I didn't. Robyn

~ 4 ~

asked me if I had ever smoked it before and I told her no, and James heard me and he said "Don't," he didn't want me to do it - a general concern - I was amazed. So, I'm cool now, ha ha - hanging out w/ James, Chris, Denise, Betsy and Lana in James' garage - oh yes. Boy wouldn't Brianna have a cow if she knew I hung out w/ him! He's a looser anyway.

!!Drove through a flood on Friday!!

Tuesday 1/23/96
I got my watch back from Rick yesterday - now we utterly have NO connection. It's amazing he hasn't talked to me in a month, yet, today I got help from Jesse (sweetie) about physics and Rick kept looking over and starring at me - he even winked. I gave him the most horrid unemotional look - he got the hint that I don't want to have anything to do with him. News Flash M.K. He's a sophomore and his hair sticks about 5 inches off his head - I love it. Whenever I think of him I smile. Well I'm hopping and feeling very dominant after watching "Disclosure" - it's about time Rick got a taste of his medicine. I am powerful, smart, beautiful, and can do anything I want! Ultimately women will control men, because we have what they want, sex!

Thursday 2/1/96
My hair is disgusting, it is an ugly yellowish green tint - and James pointed out to me how the roots were really dark. I offered to let Jesse borrow my calc notebook and he didn't want - or more so he didn't want me to drop it off at his house! I've been very upset lately and there really is no apparent reason. I'm so lonely and I really am sick of school. I am so full of hate it's overflowing through my ears. I'm mad at everything, why do things always have to end up negative. I feel ugly, stupid, and alone. I know I won't even go to the prom. Even little seventh graders make fun of me - belittle me. This is February so that means Valentine's day

is coming. Paul called me annoying - flash back to 7th grade when Jenn and Jen put a note in my locker about how not to be annoying - yeah, real cute - bitches!! Why doesn't anyone like me - Lana has a new boyfriend, Khord, from Knoll. I guess to have a boyfriend you have to have sex with them - or that's what it seems like, but no one even likes me long enough to have sex with me. What's the big deal about sex anyway, my god, it runs everyone's life - people should find a new hobby - flashback to Cole because Hobby was his best friend – jerk. But every guy can't be a jerk, it must be me - I'm a stupid air head, I have no life, no culture, I definitely don't even like myself why should anyone else. I cry all the time, I can't handle anything. I used to think it was my face, but now it's not really that bad, so maybe it's my hair, or my legs, or whatever but I don't want to have to keep making excuses for myself the rest of my life why people don't like me. I don't like me!

Friday 2/9/96

This week was horrible – I had about 10 tests, seriously. Gerard said my name in the hallway and jumped in my face. It's not a real big deal, but it's thought provoking. Rick brought about the whole Gerard thing – I had never even thought of him until Rick wanted to set me up with him, and then said that Gerard wasn't interested and yesterday at lunch Chris was kidding around and said that he heard that Gerard liked me – I'm not sure, but I think he was kidding? Then today when me and Kelly were walking in the hallway together Gerard was walking by the other way and I looked at him then leaned over to Kelly and said "isn't he cute" and Kelly said that he was watching me the whole time. I did see him out of the corner of my eye, so why did he do that? Plus now he's always walking around with stupid little albino girl. He's about 6'4"and she's about 5'4". I don't understand, me and Gerard would be perfect together, were both really tall, thin, and we both even have goofy personalities. There is nothing wrong with me, definitely not compared to albino girl – she even has a smaller chest than me, what is so appealing about her! I'm mad – we would look so good together. Also I've decided that I will not go into Kelly's house anymore – I don't feel respected there and maybe now they'll realize it's not ok to mistreat me. I miss Rick, I see him looking at me out of the corner of my eye when he thinks I'm not paying attention. I think we still have feelings for one another but there is nothing that we can do about it. Things have changed and it is as if we had never even met each other. We walk past each other in the hallway as strangers!

Saturday 2/24/96

Well, I'm basically in shock. Joanna and I went to the Knoll Dance – was pretty fun, met a guy – but it was the same one, John – so I don't know what will come of that. But the big thing is that one the way home Joanna and I got into, what turned out to be a huge fight. When I was pulling off 100 onto Farmington Ave off the ramp I didn't remember that there was (fork) and Joanna yelled at me so then I swerved onto the right side and she was thrown left. She kept yelling at me (she was in a bad mood the entire night) and so I got sick of it and stopped the car and said "get out if you don't like my driving" so she did then I drove away up to the next road and turned around and came back to pick her up, but she wouldn't get back in – so after about a half an hour I drove to Joanna's house and told her mom to go pick her up. So now I guess her and her mom hate me. I'm not really sure how she feels – she never shows any emotion at all so I don't know, we're supposed to room together in Florida and she's in all my classes! She's making me feel guilty but she was complaining all night to me and then she yelled at me. When I go to her house upset and I cry or something she tells me to stop it or go home, what's the difference? I'm mad at her for making me feel guilty – that's not fair because she never shows me any kind of compassion at all – so I do the same for her and so then she doesn't like it. Yeah she's so strong and such an individual – why should she even bother w/ me – she can just keep walking down the road right out of my life – because that's what she chose.

Sunday 3/3/96

John called me Thursday, we talked for about an hour and we got along great. I'm not sure if I'm attracted to him or not, but even if I'm not then we can become friends. He gave me his home phone #, so I'll have to call him so then we'll get together and do something, but I don't know what? Joanna and I still aren't talking! Me and Kelly have been really close lately. Grandma + Grandpa left on Thursday and I already miss them. I haven't been hungry lately – like my mind doesn't remember to eat and then my body reminds it. I hate going to Bear High, it is so ridiculous with all its little cliques. I hope college will be different. I'm not having a really great time and I'm not having a really bad time, so I guess I'm content! I saw Hunter on Friday when I was driving home from school (w/ Kelly) he was in a red Jeep Cherokee type car with what it looked like to be his mom. He saw me and I saw him – I still really do want him – a lot – mostly because he lives so close to me – I find that extremely irresistible. I feel like we belong together and that someday maybe years from now we will end up together. There is someone out there who is right for me and someday I'll find them!

Friday 3/8/96

John and I were going to go see a movie tonight with Kelly and his little brother. He said that he would call me yesterday, but he didn't, so then I finally called him at 5:00 today and he tells me that he doesn't feel that great and doesn't want to go out tonight – Fine – I said that was just fine – he apologized a lot but I'm not sure if he was sincere! School was canceled because of snow. Kelly came over and we cleaned then we went to Zerns for an hour. I wasn't really enthusiastic about John to begin with and now that he was such an idiot it just makes me even more disgusted! Ooh, a cool thing happen to me yesterday – Kevin said hi to me in the hallway – he had never talked to me before! Wow I must be hot stuff for guys I don't even know to come up to me and talk to me! P.S. Joanna and I are B.F. again!

Still Friday
I've always loved the F.B.I. Having gun and the power it holds! I've always had this incredible feeling when I go past the all boys reform institution, for really "bad" boys on 422. I picture myself being trapped in there with all those guys! Bad boys are very exciting. I want to learn karate or self defense – I want to be able to a lot of damage to a guy. I want a guy to attack me so I can teach him the lesson of his life! I know I could kill someone and get away with it! Joanna and I have talked about this before. We would never be suspected – honor students and all – it would be so easy. I would plan everything perfectly. I've also always thought of me breaking into the Knoll School wearing an all black cat suit w/ big black boots that go up to my thigh, I would have a big shotgun and so would the other 3 guys w/ me. We would be terrorists. We would wake up all the sleeping Knoll guys with a shotgun to their face. I would look perfect. One of the Knoll guys would get out of hand and I would have to put him back in his place and it would end up with my foot holding his chest down!

Sunday 3/10/96
Lana called me tonight. She is so stupid – she had absolutely nothing to talk to me about! She even put this guy on the phone w/ me that was a pot head idiot. So finally I told her that I'd had to go so she said later but I wasn't really sure so I waited and I heard her start talking about me – she is so stupid she can't even hang up the phone! she called me a bitch and said that I was a looser and had no friends! Pretty ironic if you ask me. Just add in the word slut and you would have Lana to the T. Boy, I'm going to tell Jackie,

Ken, and Carson. They all hate her too and would love to hear how stupid she is. I still feel for Hunter and don't know what to do about it?

Wednesday 3/13/96
I hate my stomach – I don't know what else I can do about it. I don't eat anything after 7:00 and I try to eat foods with no fat. I do crunches and dance. Pretty soon I'm going to skip meals all together. I need to look perfect. When Grandma and Grandpa get home I'm going to have my teeth fixed so they all look great! Can't wait! Perfection!

Saturday 3/16/96
Yesterday I went to the school play w/ Kelly – Beverly Hillbillies – Chris was so gorgeous. Then afterwards we went to High St. Hunter was there w/ Ryan. Didn't see Jason last time. I heard he had a girlfriend, but if he did then why would he be on High St. instead of w/ her? I want him to hold me – more than anyone could ever know. He is meant for me, I am stupid – Amy asked me in the beginning of my junior year if I liked him – what I thought of him – and I just basically laughed! So now it's about a year and ½ later and I have liked him now for almost a year – a whole year! I have never liked anyone that long except for Howie! He is my goal I'll do whatever it takes to be near him this summer. He is so sweet and nice. Tonight Joanna and I went to Backstreets – a dance nightclub near Kutztown College. Robin (my mother) didn't want us to go at first but then she did, surprisingly. The club was alright – too smoky, but neat. Rick was there w/ Stephanie and their little gang – ruined my whole night. All the little prep juniors were there too! How sickening. Today I got my acceptance letter from Brynell College – so I guess that's where I'm going. I hope I'll fit in – they all have so much money and I don't! I went tanning today again and got burnt very strangely on

my stomach, back and legs. Oh Hunter, I haven't a clue why I feel for you – but I do and because of that I must do something about it.

Monday 3/25/96
18 is just to old! I'm an adult now! Maturity and responsibility are words that keep popping up in my head. The senior class trip to Florida trip was alright – I got to see a lot of stuff except Joanna hung around all those dorks that I can't stand, they were nice and everything, but they weren't my style. She ignored me a lot too! (*I ended up by myself at some point in Epcot, so there I was a 17 year old girl walking around by myself. There are only two memories that I have from the entire trip. I remember being in the woods behind the park grounds when I was alone and there were other people around. It was men smoking and it looked like people hung out there because there was litter on the ground. The other memory I have is from when all of us on the class trip went to Medieval Times. We ripped the hen apart and had to eat it with our hands. During the jousting they choose a girl to be the princess to fight over and I didn't understand why they choose the girl they did? Later we found out she was having sex with the school counselor that was on the trip so it was all clearly rigged.*)* I got really mad over the Florida trip and yelled at Chris and Ken about making fun of my name and today in the library they said "Hi Mawwy" and I looked at them then turned away – they got the hint. Hunter is still on my mind a lot! I got a lot of GAP stuff – I look a lot older and worldly in them! Happy Birthday to me! eighteen wow!

Tuesday 3/26/96
Kristen said that she had talked to Jarred today, Hunter's little brother. Kristen asked him if his brother was single and he said "ya, but he won't go out with Mary." How did he know! Why wouldn't he want to at least date me – I'm not that bad. He was my only fantasy whenever a love song would come on the radio or

I saw a couple on TV I would think of him! I feel like crying or yelling but I can't, he never was mine, ever, to begin with, but eight little words just changed all my dreams. I wish I could be ignorant and unknowing like an innocent little child – nothing would be complicated or have consequences. I have nothing to look forward to at all – no hope, so much of my life has been wasted by loneliness – I want to be loved – cared for in that way, why would anyone feel for me! Is it my fault? Is it my appearance? I want to yell at him – hit him, anything, how dare he make me feel like this – he has no right. Everyone controls my life except me. I am so dependent on others thoughts – I have no mind!

Saturday 3/29/96

There was a Knoll dance tonight – was really cool – had a RAVE room were me and Joanna spent the whole night. Joanna met this really cute preppie – Ryan. I went in the hallway because it was so hot. This guy grabbed my hand and asked me to dance – I lied and said I wasn't a good dancer because I figured that he would just want to grind and use me. So then we went outside where a whole bunch of people were outside the door and talked for over a half an hour. He was so cool and said "I love you," he liked me so much – I was loving it! Then John walked by – and later realized it was me, and then they were joking around about who gets me + then they started to pretend to have a dual w/ swords – fighting over me, and I jumped in the middle to stop them and John pushed me back saying that I'll get stabbed. I kind of feel bad for John but Bobby is so cool. I was so happy we kidded around like we had known each other 5 years. I was so free w/ him – not self-conscience at all. He said that me and Joanna were "fuckin' awesome" – and yes I agree. Bye Bye John – Hello Bobby.

Tuesday 4/2/96

Yesterday Bobby called me, he only waited one day – he must

really like me. He is so nice and he gave me his phone # and said that he is looking forward to every second talking with me, and that he will be waiting day and night for my call! I think I'll call him tomorrow. Today I stayed home from school to type my research paper –

Friday 4/5/96

I wrecked my room frantically looking for the one picture I had had of Cole. I've now determined that I ripped it up or through it out in a folder. I want to see that picture so bad! Bobby is away partying for Easter! I am non-important once again. The only thing I'm looking forward to is having my teeth stripped (or something) so then they will all be one color – yes! 4/22 can't wait. I was really looking forward to seeing Bobby tonight or tomorrow, but I should have known. I called him a bunch of times this week and he thought it was Mary Kate, I don't even know who she is, but he called her back, he didn't even remember me. I'm nothing to no one! Great, well I was all excited to go to the Knoll Prom, but now I won't, and I'm not even going to my own prom. He'll probably of forgotten me by Tuesday and I'll never hear from him again. The sad part is that I am truly going to be right

Monday 4/8/96

On Saturday night Joanna and I went to Backstreets. We saw Maxamillion live he sings the song sexual healing and fat boy – that was cool. Also I came home at 1:30am – which because of the change in the time was actually 2:30am – so that was a first. Well I wonder if Bobby will ever call me back. Kelly and I are going to call Knoll tomorrow and find out when the next home tennis game is – so I guess we will go and see what happens.

Tuesday 4/8/96

Today I had an accident – all my fault. I rear-ended April on the off ramp going to school (doin' it was on the radio by LL Cool J, song drives me nuts). April was really cool about it. I feel really bad and my head is starting to hurt a lot. Bobby didn't call me still – I feel horrible – he seemed to like me so much and it just faded! I don't understand. I had so much stress, and my period is late for the second month in a row – I'm not sure if I should be concerned or not. I've been thinking and the Knoll School gets out for summer in the middle of May so then Bobby will only be here for a month and a half! Then I guess I'm back to hounding Hunter? Jarred knows I like him.

Wednesday 4/10/96
I called Jenn for the 3rd night in a row and we talked for a long time – I felt better talking to her cause I've known her for so long and we decided that we would get together sometime then I called Bobby, but he wasn't there and I talked to Jeremy – the guy I had meet at Taco Bell earlier! Well then Bobby called me back – I was very happy. He said that he was all excited that I called and we talked for a long time. He wants me to come to his tennis matches – cool. But he also said that John has been asking about me!- also that the reason that John ditched me before was because he got flyers tickets! He wasn't sick! And Bobby said that I should go to John's lacrosse games – Boy I'm confused, why would Bobby tell me to do that? He said that John was hot for my body! So I don't know what I want to do? I told Bobby that I don't want to go. Ooh Bobby also said that maybe me and John could rekindle our relationship – so I'm not sure what's going on. I'm so surprised that John is asking about me – I told Bobby to tell him hi for me? Well I feel better anyway.

Sunday 4/14/96
I was so sick this weekend my throat hurt, my head ached; I couldn't even walk up my steps. I guess it's because of all the stress this week w/ the accident and all. I'm not going to go to school tomorrow. I should work on my research paper. I also

have a calc test on Tuesday and I have to make up a physics test I FAILED – wonderful – can't wait until summer! Then I'll have to get a job – great!!!!!

Wednesday 4/17/96
Yesterday night Bobby called me. I was really surprised – he wanted to make sure that I was going to his tennis match. Kelly and I went today – we had a great time. At first I couldn't remember what he looked like but then Kelly waved to him later and he came over and talked to us. Afterwards Kelly, me, Bobby, Jeremy, and Juan + his two Spanish friends went over to Boston Market to eat. They were so funny and Bobby + Jeremy kept drooling all over everything. Also Lynda (my best friend from 9th grade) was working there, they all thought that she was hot – I was kind of jealous. Anyway Jeremy is really hot, but Bobby is really nice, and also Juan was sweet and he remembered me. Had a fun day – I needed one.

Sunday 4/21/96
Yesterday I went over to Knoll to watch another tennis match. Bobby lost, Jeremy won, and I had absolutely no fun! But it was weird, because then Bobby called me at around 8:00 and while he was talking to me Jeremy walked by and then got on the phone and said how he needed somewhere to be for the next couple of hours. So then Jeremy and Bobby came over! It was weird for me. I feel like I needed to entertain them or something, I think they were pretty bored! Grandma liked them a lot and they seemed to like her very much so also. Grandma gave them Amish friendship bread and they were shoving it in their mouths so fast that they couldn't even talk. I guess they enjoyed home life for two hours; it probably was a nice change for them from boarding school!

Thursday 4/25/96
On Monday I called Bobby to tell him how Gina talked to me at

lunch. He had to go for a meeting, and then he called me back at around 10:30. We talked for a while and I felt really good inside. Then the next day, Tuesday, I got a phone call at 10:40, I was sound asleep and I thought it was Bobby – but it was John! I haven't talked to him in a long time. I liked talking to him. I really liked talking to him a lot, a lot more than Bobby! But now I can't even call John because I don't have his dorm #. I'm so lonely, Bobby ignores me anyway – never asks me to do anything! John is so big and strong – I want him now! I was going to call any dorm and ask when the next lacrosse game was so then I could see him, but all the phones were busy! I want someone so bad. I'm beginning to feel so horrible – everyone is talking about the prom and buying dresses. Joanna is even probably going - w/ stupid dork BM and tomorrow is Junior Dinner Dance, so all the Juniors get to leave early. When do I get my chance for anything! He didn't call me! My existence is pathetic in all possible forms.

Friday 4/26/96
Well I finally tracked down John's dorm #, so then I was going to call him and ask him to go to the prom, but then he didn't come to the phone and I swear I heard him talking to the kid that answered the phone. So then Kelly called and asked for him and the kid said, oh he can't talk right now! Ah ha! So then I called Bobby and asked him to go w/ me but he couldn't because he has a train ticket. But we talked for a real long time and he is supposed to come over tomorrow night! I guess I'll have to call John sometime and see if he'll go with – if he can't then I'm screwed. Joanna is going, and I want to too!

Saturday 4/27/96
Bobby came over – he even gave up going to a party for me – whoa. He was really sweet and he loved to make conversation w/ my grandparents. He was pretty nosey though – but that's cool because I'm just like that too! Anyway I told him that the

handshake thing wasn't cool so then he finally kissed me! I was pleased – can't wait till the Dance next week – Yum yum!

Sunday 4/28/96

I've never been so scared and tense in my whole life – I feel like I'm just about to give a speech to about a million people. I'm going to call John and ask him to the prom – what if he won't come to the phone or even worse says NO to me! I'm so scared; my fate depends on the call! Aaaah! (He said Yes!!!)

Sunday 5/5/96

Yesterday was my last dance at the Knoll School – the Spring Fling! I didn't even see Bobby the whole night, so I spent most of the night w/ John and we danced the last slow song together! I went over to the lacrosse and tennis match – yes both. Kelly was laughing hysterically at me because I had to keep walking back and forth between them. I would watch John play for a little then walk over and watch Bobby play; I took Bobby and Jeremy the Amish Friendship Bread. John lost his game and he was really upset – he came over and talked to me afterwards and I told him that I would bring him some Amish Friendship Bread at the dance – and I did. I was so upset Bobby wasn't there – or so I thought. But when I got home Grandpa told me that Bobby had called me right after I left and was looking for me! So Grandpa told him that "I went out" – Dork – so Bobby thought that I didn't go!!! I called Bobby this morning, but he was at breakfast and he called me back later when the neighbors Candy and Lucas were here. We talked and straightened everything out – he said that we'll probably get together next weekend. I really like Bobby a lot but I know he's leaving and I have to keep my options open especially since John is going to the prom w/ me. Ooh so Gavin said to Bobby – "Ooh I heard that Mary ditched you for John to go to the prom!" – Bobby told me on the phone- we both laughed – I think that's hysterical. Anyway John and I were really close and things are getting sticky

– how am I going to handle both of them for a month. Also I had a regressive day – Lucas, Candy and I played lacrosse for an hour or so and then we all went to Douglass Park – Candy and I played on the playground and on the swings. Then Joanna, Candy, and I all went for a bike ride down to the woods and we walked down the stream to a fallen tree and it was so peaceful. I love being a kid again – I wish I could be like that every day!

Sunday 5/12/96

I found out that I mean nothing to Bobby. Friday night Kelly and I went over to Knoll to stop by and just say Hi! I was wearing my Indian head dress and Kelly was wearing my pirates of the Caribbean hat – we were in a really goofy mood – all hyper and stuff – but then the Knoll people were so mean to us – they said, NO Bobby wasn't here – then said "let me go check" – never came back, then some other guy said he was a teacher and said that Bobby was there – he never came back – then the other guy came back and said that he went to a prom! Ya sure, after Bobby told me how much he hates proms and thinks that they are stupid, also his parents don't allow him to leave campus – and even if they had – the Knoll boys aren't allowed to leave on Friday nights anyway because they have school the next day and furthermore – the guy that told us that Bobby went to the Prom didn't even bother to ask who we were – as if he already knew! Not to mention the fact that I saw people up in the windows as we were leaving. Gee, do I smell a liar or two! He doesn't care – I'm almost 100% certain. I know that he will not call but every time the phone rings I still get a little tingle up my spine that it might be him. I don't like to feel worthless – especially because of someone I never intended to meet or even talk to – someone I tried to get rid of but was unsuccessful at doing so. I'm mad – mad as hell! How dare I be treated like this – I deserve better than those spoiled brats – if I ever see Bobby again, which I doubt, I don't know what I will do – I try not to make a fool of myself but when anger strikes there are no prisoners. He was in my room touching my things, and every time I look around my room I see something that he had looked at, and bam – he's in my head. This is not fair – but then I just remember – what goes around comes around!

Saturday 5/19/96
He called me on Saturday – Bobby called me after I had forgotten about him – when the phone rang before I was certain that it wasn't him – no flinch in my mind, but now the flinch is back. I do wish that I could of seen him this weekend – he probably wanted me to come pick him up, but that's not fair to me that he only thinks of me when it's convenient for him or he has nothing else to do. I think that it was the last time he will call because I feel so empty inside. I can still remember his voice and his face. Life is pretty strange – things happen when you least expect them to and things turn out so much different then what you thought. Jason and I are talking w/ each other and becoming friends. He looks at me a certain way and I can just tell that there is more to his eyes than meets the eye. Maybe he wonders why nothing ever happened between us (we went to Harvest Ball together in the fall) – or maybe he's just thinking to himself but whatever it is, it definitely has something to do w/ him and I when we look at each other, I know he knows. They always come back; they always like me again no matter how much they try not to! By God they always come back – always!!

Sunday 5/26/96
This weekend has been pretty cool! On Friday night John came up and then Joanna and I followed him up to Eagle. I saw his house and we went to a party at this kid Dan's house. His house was beautiful – so big w/ an indoor hot tub. John was pretty drunk for most of the night. He was all over me – he even did the firemen carry to me – that's cool though because I always wanted to be, I guess the word is submissive. We had a lot of fun, some of the

guys who were there were Rob, Zack, Andrew, Meat, and of course Dan "Pouck" the person who's house it was – I liked him – I liked him a lot – he was really nice and he wasn't drinking like all the other guys. I know he had to of remembered me from the dances because we made eye contact so many times! Joanna was interested in him and I think he was interested in her too but I can't help but think that if John wasn't all over me he would have talked to me a lot more, we looked into each other's eyes so much – and you don't make that kind of eye contact with no feeling behind it. Dan said to me that the next time I was over at John's house he would stop by. Strange that he said that. Also when we left he was upset because we weren't sleeping over and he wouldn't shake my hand in a kidding sort of way – but then I took his hand and told him what a great time I had and how nice his house was and he seemed content. I know where he lives and I would love to visit him this summer – maybe I just might do that. Anyway last night Bobby came over and I had forgotten how wonderful he really is and now that I think about it I am extremely upset that he is leaving – I feel so sad. When he came over it was hysterical, we sat and watched T.V. for a while but then we both knew that we wanted to be alone so we left early and drove to Pottstown and parked on the side of some street in front of all these row homes. He turned to me and said in a sweet way "kiss me" and I said "whatever you say" and that's when the fun started. We jumped into the back seat and started kissing but then I heard voices and there were people walking by so we ducked down behind the seats and I was laughing so hard – we were like little junior high kids. So then we were "making out" in the back seat and it was so much fun – I never felt so secure w/ myself and my body w/ anyone before – I was even giving him instruction! We are so open w/ each other. I could tell him anything – we were hot and heavy for about 20 minutes and boy I was out of breath! He was kissing me so hard that my lips were chapped when I got home – not to mention that they were already burnt from the 10 mile bike ride

Joanna and I had gone on earlier that day, but anyway Bobby got offended w/ me because I thought he thought that we were going to have sex and I accused him of that and he was really upset so then he just laid his head on my stomach and we talked. He asked me if I had ever had sex before and I told him no. He was surprised but also confessed that he was a virgin too and I thought that was so sweet, I don't think he was lying, but it has crossed my mind. We both laid there for a couple minutes and talked about him leaving while I stroked his head that was lying on my stomach. I drove him over to Knoll and he asked me for a kiss goodbye – he also asked for a picture and with big grins on both of our faces we said goodbye and that we'd call each other. I never intended to meet Bobby, but I'm so glad I did. Saying goodbye will be hard but I really want to stay friends and I'll put my address on the back of my picture. If he was staying longer or whatever – I know I could fall in love w/ him – but I guess it just wasn't meant to be that way – for now! I'll never forget Bobby – what we have to me is so special that we could go off in our separate ways and still be friends even when were both married to other people – that's what I'm hoping for in the future – just a friend, perhaps a lover.

Tuesday 5/28/96
People must always be thinking about something – I was wondering if anyone was thinking about me and I pictured people in the hallway walking by me at school and each and every one of them must be thinking about something - Jason was talking to me today in 9th period – I can tell by his eyes when he talks to me- he's thinking about what he's saying and taking in my reactions. We both want each other and I think we both know it too – the thing is though are we willing to tell each other – I will soon maybe at the prom or after graduation. This summer I will get a job somewhere and be productive! Everything is changing so fast that my head is spinning – Not to mention the fact that the Chinese food that Joanna, Kelly and I had doesn't help much.

Sunday 6/2/96

Friday night was the Prom!! Bobby is in New Hampshire now.
We talked Thursday night and said goodbye. He is nice and I'm
truly glad that I met him. The days go by so fast and everything is
changing. High School will be over in 5 days. Crying is pretty
much a daily ritual right now. I'm so confused. Everyone at the
prom said how good John and I looked together, but I don't know.
All I could think about was Jason, Wolf, and Bobby. By the end of
the prom Wolf called me Mare – like we were old friends – I could
marry him – he's just that type. I had fun at the prom and John
slept over – he saw me w/o make up in the morning and he still
likes me – wow. I will miss Joanna dreadfully when college starts.
I will be all alone. I will have no friends! The first month will be
horrible. What am I going to do all summer! I have nothing to do
at all. I guess I'll have to get a job and stuff, but I just don't know.
I'll never see Carson, Brendon, or Hans or Jason again. They'll be
off into their destiny which I won't be a part of. How saddening
life can be. This is the end of my childhood forever – now I have
to become an adult.

Sunday 6/9/96

On Friday was graduation – was o.k., nothing big. Joanna's
grandmother upset me – so I called John, we decided that I would
come over on Sunday (today) and I would bring the promenade so
him and his mom could see. This morning John called at around
10:30am woke me up and started yelling at me that I called at
1:00am that morning – of course I didn't and was all confused –
still don't know who really called. So I went over at 3:30 and met
his mom, step-dad, and little brothers. We took a 3 mile walk
through the woods and ended up at a real big lake then walked
back on the road. It was pleasant. Then we went out to eat and he
said he would feel a lot better if he showed me where he used to
live so we went. He made me wear my seatbelt because he was
going around 70 on these windy roads. Then we went back to his

house and hung out w/ his little brothers for a while then he told me I had to leave – I said see ya and he said the same so don't know what's up with that. He made me feel disgusting – he never wanted to look at me or touch me I'm not really expecting a call back from him! Any way this weekend was Fun Days at the Park. Robin saw Jason and told him to call me – and he did tonight – the next day – that same night after I got home from John's.

Wednesday 6/12/96
Today was my 1st day at work at Pop's Restaurant. It was horrible, I basically did nothing and got in the way. I don't like it at all – they were less than inviting. I didn't even answer the phone because I was scared I would screw up. I miss Jason. He came over on Monday from 1:30pm to 10:00pm. We rollerbladed, then went swimming, sat on the deck at Kelly's house and talked – he was really cool, then we came over to my house for dinner – turkey – and later had pizza w/ Kelly and Kristen. I loved being w/ him and he kissed me at the end of the night – he grabbed my butt and pulled me into him – I was gleefully surprised, I thought he was the passive type – I like sexually aggressive dominating men! Today he (Jason) went to Kutztown for a 2 day orientation. He called me yesterday to talk and said he'll call Thursday night when he gets home from Kutztown. I can't wait to see him I guess I'll see him either Sunday night or Monday. I want him – Yum Yum. This is weird – we didn't even talk for 5 months strait after Thanksgiving when we went to the Harvest Ball together – in time I'll ask him about that, definitely!

Tuesday 6/18/96
Jason? He seems to be the main topic in my life right now. Well I went to see him Friday night after work – which by the way is much better now – Jeremy, the manager, is so funny - anyway we watched at movie and goofed around, it was nice. Then yesterday I went over to Jason's at 12:40pm to rollerblade – Hans came over

then he drove us in the jeep over to the high school and we all skated around in the parking lot. Boy is Hans buff! Anyway then after work we went out to see "The Cable Guy" and that was also nice – we saw Wolf and Jesse there too – Wolf is so cute. So after the movie I stayed over Jason's house for about an hour and talked in the driveway for a while. He's only kissed 5 girls and I've kissed ten guys – double his, wow. Well, I guess I like him. I didn't see him or talk to him at all today and I kind of missed him, but that worries me because I don't want to become too attached because we're both going to college in the fall and even though our colleges are only a half an hour or so apart, that still would never work because college is a new beginning and you leave the past behind! His parents are leaving tomorrow and it will be interesting to see what happens! Though last night we didn't end on such good terms – he always gets upset w/ me – I don't think it will last at all – not even to July. All we do is make fun of each other, and he rates me a 7 on a scale of ten (he rates himself a 6) – I don't know if I want to be a 7 when I could find some other guy that thinks I'm a 10!!! I was really depressed this morning, I couldn't get up and I was so hungry the entire day! I went over Kelly's and watched "Now and Then" and it was good. I also went to see Joanna tonight. I haven't seen her since Saturday which is really long considering we see each other at least twice a day. I'm very sad and I don't really know why and that scares me! P.S. Brynell is stupid – people are dorky – visited Saturday – oh what fun!

Thursday 6/20/96
Yesterday Jason called after I had driven by his house w/ Kelly and Kristen – make sure he wasn't having fun w/o me! – no one was home. When I got home though, he called and said he was at the Loan Star w/ friends, I was relieved, so then he asked me to come over and I did. We spent a lot of time talking and too much for him – he wasn't too thrilled w/ me talking and was hinting that "we" wouldn't work out so then I got mad – grabbed his hand and

~ 24 ~

drug him into his bedroom – I told him to lie down, I blew out the candle then straddled myself on top of him. Needless to say – he was pleased! I had fun to – it was kind of like having sex w/ our clothes on – or as Kristen would say "dry humping." He called me again tonight and wanted me to come over but it was already 11:00 and that's too late. Gee I wonder what we'll do when I see him tomorrow. His parents left yesterday and are gone for nine days – which I think is really cool! We're becoming closer as the days go by – I am sure he likes me, maybe even more than I think!

Friday 6/21/96
I went over Jason's tonight – because Hans was leaving Jason decided to throw him a going away party which was hysterical because Hans got really drunk and kept throwing up all over the place – I spent about 20 min. scratching/rubbing his head – I felt bad for him because he was so sick – it made Jason jealous that I was scratching his head (Hans did wait for me outside homeroom that one time, I know he wanted to date me) anyway Jason and I had another long discussion about what we like or what we should do – or whatever. He ended up telling me that he liked me a lot – which in a way surprises me. I like him too and everyday I think I grow to like him more – he has many flaws – but so do I and I think that makes us good for each other – though he's not conscience of his flaws and I am!

Sunday 6/23/96
Today I worked – as usual and I worked yesterday – as usual – and Jason came over for a little while yesterday – kind of unusual – I went over Jason's house after work tonight – as usual. Kevin was there – Jason's best bud. We all sat around and talked for a while – they were both putting back beers then it got cold and we all went inside. Kevin poured me a shot of some kind of whiskey and then a couple more after that – I was a little out of it, I never drank alcohol before. Then Jason led me back into the bedroom for a

little make out session or whatever. After about 20-25 min Kevin came back and was kidding around that he wanted to watch – ya ok, whatever then he wanted to join in – I was out of it and Jason didn't care – so then he did – I feel so horrible – I am a whore, slut, hoe – whatever – and tonight we had just determined that we were boyfriend and girlfriend – and here I am w/ Kevin. Ooh – what am I going to do – a lot of stuff happened – stuff I hadn't done before – well actually one thing I hadn't done before – but it wasn't Jason who did it to me it was Kevin – Ooh Ooh Ooh – I feel horrible – I hate myself so much right now.

Wednesday 6/26/96
The days go by so fast, in exactly two months I'll be at college. Well after the Sunday night incidence – Kevin flipped out – Jason told me that Kevin hates me and couldn't stand to be in the same room w/ me w/ out punching me in the face because he has a girlfriend– he said it was all my fault. So now I can't even see Jason because Kevin's having a huge party Friday night and I'm not invited now because I might upset Kevin. What the Fuck? See, I knew it wasn't a good idea – at least I learned my lesson for good – never again – never! I don't know – I'm all confused – do I like Jason or don't I? Things are changing fast! College – how am I ever going to handle that?

Saturday 6/29/96
Well Jason invited me to come over after work, so I did. Then when I was over I kept smelling my hands, they smelt like hoagies and he came over and sat next to me and agreed. Then he kept saying how bad I smelled and I asked him if he wanted me to take a shower – he said no so I told him to shut up about and he didn't – so then I left – I came home – took a shower!! – called up Joanna and took my old Halloween mask and went on up to Jason's. See he gets real scared when he's alone so I figured this would be great, we would scare him – but the dork was asleep and all the

doors were locked – so we turned all the furniture on the patio over – and also his bike – maybe he'll find it tomorrow and be freaked out. Also I took a broom and banged it against his window about 5 times – still no reaction and before that I was scratching my nails down all his screens – nothing. But then when we were standing in front of his house his parents pulled into the fucking driveway, ooh my, so we were skitzing! We ran behind a bush and hid w/ headlights right on us and then we crawled across the yard into the neighbors yard behind a tree – Joanna grabbed my arm and we ran to the car that was parked in a ditch on the side of the road – then we were hiding behind the car because his parents were still in the driveway – I ran over to my side of the car and opened it but Joanna couldn't get in on her side so she had to climb in over my side while I was pushing her to go as fast as she could – it was hysterical – absolutely hysterical like from a movie or something – we drove off w/ the headlights off – both our hearts exploding from our chests – then w/ such a rush we went to High St. We meet these guys and went to McDonalds and talked to them – they were really funny and I told them about Jason and how me and Joanna went to scare Jason when he was home alone – they all thought it was really funny. Then we went for a drive around "the block" in their really cool white mustang car – I was squished in the back – Joanna had shotgun – they were funny but they were really old – like 21-22, I can't even remember. But it was nice to vent – but now I want Jason – Joanna keeps telling me that he is such a looser and that he uses me and is a dick to me – well if he uses me then I use him right back – I definitely get mine – I hope things don't go sour – I would seriously miss him – and all his imperfections – there are a lot! If he doesn't call me soon then I'll call him. Ya, and all he did after I left is go to sleep – Ha Ha Ha Ha Ha Ha Ha Ha Ha Ha

Tuesday 7/2/96

Jason and I are still – should I say together – but we haven't been seeing very much of each other lately – we talked on the phone today and he said that we could spend the whole day Friday together – but why does he want to wait until Friday? Ooh well – I know he works a lot this week but that never stopped him before – I miss him – maybe not even really him – just the idea of him more so – I miss being held and hugged. Jason and I really aren't very compatible. Ashley B. had a kind of birthday party tonight – I was over their house while they were getting ready and Jamie was talking to me – he said that some guy Joe on his baseball league said that I was doing everything but fucking Jason – what? He said the kid went to some private school (catholic) and that I would never know him – I just don't know if he was lying or what – maybe I'll have to ask Jason about this but I think I'll talk to Jamie again first. After Ashley's party Kelly and I picked up Joanna and went to the Norco fair were we meet up w/ Adrian. We all went on the salt and pepper shakers together – it was hysterical – I felt so dizzy – my head hurt bad! Then Joanna and I went on the tilt-a-whirl that was fun too after we got bored w/ the fair we went over to High St – but there was no one there so we went to Diary Queen and ate then on High St we saw these guys in a red convertible and then later they pulled over and waited for us. They were older, and the driver, Brian was really HOT, the other two were pretty ugly – but the one guy Will took my # and said he would call me at 5:00 tomorrow to tell us about some kind of party. Kelly said that they were drug dealers – probably so – but ooh well – connections are always good. It will be interesting to see what happens tomorrow! Sometimes I feel like I'm really a big slut inside but my imperfections prevent me from acting on my instinct – boy if everything was perfect about me – I definitely would be a major HO!

Thursday 7/4/96

Went over Jason's tonight – we were kind of fooling around and we were talking about THAT Sunday (w/ Kevin) and Jason said that he seriously thought we were going to have sex – he really wanted to and he even told me that that was why he was trying so hard to get my panties off. He said that his goal was to get me completely naked! Darn, if Kevin wasn't there who knows? I want him so bad – especially because he is a virgin too, and I know I'll meet a guy at college and everything but he'll have already had 5 or so girls and I don't want to be another # - not at all. I want him so bad – I think about him every night before I go to bed – and at least 20 times during the day – his birthday is Sunday and this morning I went out and bought him cute preppie GAP clothes. I will seduce him – I will get what I want! I always get what I want – I wanted him – I have him! He is the only guy I've ever known to refuse sex! I'll wear him down! I will have him! He even said what he likes to do is turn the girl on – please her – that's what turns him on, how sweet! My summer goal has been established.

Sunday 7/14/96

Been working – new guy at work Rob – wants me real bad – he touches me all the time – grabs my butt and everything – worse than Jose. They all want me at work – even Josh the Delivery person was being just a little too flirty the other day. Work is fun when there is flirting going on! Jason and I are still together. We went to the mall on Wed. and he stayed over my house for a little while afterwards and today I went over to see him, his mom was having a "kind of" party for him – but when I got there after work everyone had left. Jason's – hmm – what's the word? I don't know but I'm smiling so what's the difference. Joanna and I went rollerblading on High St last night – that was COOL! Life is fun!

Friday 7/19/96

Saw Jason this afternoon – taunted him – he gets so frustrated.
Went rollerblading w/Joanna after dinner. In a week I leave for the
shore! That means that I only have 5 more weeks till school starts
and I can only see Jason for 3 of those weeks and I usually see him
twice a week that means I'll only see him 6 more times – and just
now when I realized this I started crying. I wonder if he'll want to
keep in touch or not – I know there will be no type of boyfriend –
girlfriend relationship between us when college starts – I know he
wouldn't want that and I'm not sure that I would either. The more
I think about it college is going to be horrible – I will be so lonely.
Ooh Jeremiah called me last night, he is really strange – he wanted
me to come over sometime and I just thought that he was being so
weird – he said love ya at the end of our conversation - who
knows?

Monday 7/22/96

I am bored w/ life – keep trying to think of exciting things to do.
Tonight Kelly, Kristen and I went out and then went to High St.
and I felt like taking my shirt off and driving around in my bra –
not many people noticed but the people who did showed a strong
interest! I saw Jason on Saturday, he ignored me for about 2 hr
and then he turned the T.V. off and things heated up. Let's just say
that when I left he was still shaking like a leaf. Today we were
supposed to go to the movies – but Hans came back for some
college boards – so they spent the day together. Jason is confusing
– he is so sarcastic – I don't even think he even likes me let alone
cares for me! He better wise up. I'm definitely – at the shore.

Monday 7/29/96

Joanna and I have been at the shore for three days now. Let's
review the highlights of these days - sat we saw two guys on
rollerblades pointing at our house – then thought we saw that kid
Dan from last year - went to club 2 – sucked but meet Tom who

was really nice On Sunday we saw Mark + Jay T. – Tony P. and
Joanna met a Canadian guy in a T-shirt store. Today we went
rollerblading instead of going to the beach – we went to the board
walk and got a whoopee coushin w/ my coupons. Had fun making
farting sounds on the boardwalk for four hours. Saw cloths I want
to buy at the boardwalk mall. Meet two guys on rollerblades that
want to skate w/ us tomorrow! Was invited to a party at the
admiral – room 718. We went and no one was there so we left.
On the way home saw guys on bikes – talked to them. The shore
has been pretty fun. No lifeguards – well one – has talked to me
(he was a dork) beats me? Wonder how Jason and Kelly are? I'll
send each of them a postcard soon. Though I do miss Jason – Ooh
Grandma has a nurse friend whose son goes to Brynell and is a
Junior and said that him and his friends can help me move into my
dorm. His name is Tim S. – that'll be so awesome! I can become
friends w/ the upperclassman guys – I hope everything works out –
that'll be so perfect – I'm excited now! I'll miss good old Jason,
going to his party college? Wonder what the future holds?

Thursday 8/1/96
Today was interesting. The Hunton's came – they were funny –
then after dinner Joanna and I went to the boards. Two Christian
follower people talked to us for a half an hour – wasted our guy
hunting time, then two guys came up to us at a bench and said how
we farted at them the other night! Their names were Bob and
Kevin. Then they said some of their friends – who also
remembered me and the whoopee cushion this one kid Mike was
so cool –he was short but his personality made up for it – he was
awesome and I want him – he was talking to me and he put his arm
around my waste – I know he wanted me and they all know my
name was Mary because Mike told them and it was really cool but
Bob liked me so I couldn't be w/ Mike. Bob is really cute – but he
doesn't float my boat – I don't really know why but he is cute –
we're supposed to go see them tomorrow at around 1:00am – ya

right - but we will go and I do want to get really drunk so hello Mr. Beer can!

Saturday 8/3/96
Jack C.! Joanna and I went to the boards after the Huntons surprise party (50th Anv.) We met two wonderful guys. He was so nice – but he had to leave the very next day – I'm glad we meet them. Joanna is going to go rollerblading w/ Jason. Joanna really liked Jason – too bad Jack isn't staying – oh and we lost the car! What a night

Sunday 8/4/96
Joanna is fucking wasted! Today was unbelievable. This morning Joanna went w/ Jason rollerblading. She told me at the beach that he was really weird – tried to force himself on her – well he tried to kiss and she didn't like that idea. Well we went to the boards and about 10 mins after this guy came up to us at a bench – Brian pre-med, Temple – we set up a time – 11:00 – to met him at his house. While we were walking back Jason spotted us – had to talk to him for a while – Jason said Jack said that I was really attractive and that if he could spend another week here he would be in heaven! They were talking about that in Italian when we were walking to the car. Anyway we went to this guy's house and he had Everclear – 95% alcohol 190 proof. Joanna took a big gulp full – more than he had – I had a little gulp. It was funny – Joanna was fine while we were in his place – but as soon as we got in our car – Joanna told me that she was wasted – and she was and still is while I'm sitting here right next to her – I had to told her up in the room – she fucking fell over 4 times! She is drunk, totally drunk – what she drank is equivalent to about 8 or 10 beers – surprised she's not throwing up yet – I was a little buzzed but I really had to keep under control so that I could keep her from looking like a fool – Gee I wonder what Grandma and Grandpa are going to do

tomorrow – wonder if they're going to say anything to us? Surfing
tomorrow 6:30 –

Monday 8/5/96
Went to beach – had fun – took a walk on the beach in my string
bikini – talked to the life guards I always talk to (the only life
guards I talk to – by choice) Marty and Dave L. They were
hilarious Marty especially – We were talking about Jason and
being ravaged and dominated then they both started getting really
excited – it was hilarious. Then it turned out that Dave and I got
hooked up – I rollerbladed over to this house and, well, and then a
lot. His was really nice though never did anything I didn't want
him to – we played a strip game and he lost – nice body - -he said I
had "nice tits" – which I take as a great compliment. He wanted to
have sex but when I told him that I was a virgin he said he could
never do that – how sweet! We fooled around for a little and then
we did something new (for me) "titty fucking" – didn't think I was
equipped enough but it worked out. I got a "ring of pearls" or
"pearl necklace." I didn't feel used or bad about what I did – and I
think that is good (Dave is easily 15 years older than me). Ooh ya
– Joanna and I went over to see Brian again later – he's nice – butt
ugly though!

Friday 8/9/96
There is much to say about the last two days! On Thursday
afternoon I went for my walk along the beach to talk to Marty. On
the way back another lifeguard talked to me & his name was Mike
and we made plans to get together later – he happened to live in the
lifeguard house on 24th and N.Y. – the party house – So I ended up
going over (after Ben + Matt from last year stopped by). I
rollerbladed over because Joanna didn't want to go so I couldn't
take the car. Mike turned out to be a real dork and I figured that he
night would be a big letdown. Chip and I were talking and he was
interested in how I knew about the house and I told him about

Daniel. Then Chip told me that he still lived there – and my heart
fluttered – hope for the evening had sparked, first to see him again
would have been wonderful – Marty had said that he never heard
of a Daniel. Less than 15 min. later Daniel walks in the door w/
his body board. His hair was much shorter – the fro was gone and
he was still incredibly cute – But I was stuck w/ this guy Mike!
Daniel remembered me and talked to me in a way that we were old
friends. Daniel and Mike walked into the kitchen and talked then
later Daniel asked me to join him skateboarding on my rollerblades
– which I of course did – not considering Mike for an instant, but it
didn't matter because I found out later (while we were
rollerblading) that Daniel asked Mike if he wouldn't mind if he
and I spent time together. He told Mike that he had meet me last
year and suggested that I was, in a way, special to him. So we
went out rollerblading from 8:00pm to 12:30pm. We talked and he
tried to do stunts. Then we went down towards the bay and sat on
a bench and talked – a lighted one (we got yelled at earlier) before
he had taken off his shoes and socks and ran down into the ocean
because he felt sweaty and gross. We talked about high school and
Jason, about dating and his love for reading. He wants to be an
English teacher. When it was about time for me to leave he said
that he had to see more of me – and he said that I could sneak out
or that he would sneak in but it didn't work out too well. The door
was jammed – Grandpa wouldn't fall asleep and I was making a
racket. I finally decided to crawl out the kitchen window and
hopefully see him out there – which I did. He told me that he had
tried to crawl through the window but when he was half way
through Grandpa came out of his bedroom and turned the
bathroom light on. So he and I drove back to his place. He told
me that he had told Chip that he was going on a "mission." –
which was cute – and he had never done anything like that before.
We got to his house and went up to his room – the whole house
was dark. We talked for a while – he told me he had a diary – just
like me! He was so perfect and being near him made me nervous

and I started shaking – plus the fact that I was cold added to the embarrassing shiver. We are so much alike and everything just flowed so smoothly. Everything I like he did. He took his shirt off first, then he took my tank top off and unhooked my bra that was soon to be off also. Both bare chested with our bodies pressed up against each other – was wonderful. I love a lot of contact. We were kissing and joking and giggling – we got along so well. Then he took his shorts off and then mine. The only clothing between the two of us was my panties. His body was perfectly placed on top of mine as if they were adjoining pierce of a puzzle. We were engulfed with each other, flesh to flesh. I had never felt the pure physical sensations that I was feeling. The blood rush out of my head and my hands convulsively clenched into fists that the jaws of life could not open. Long passionate kisses in between heavy petting, I felt like I was going to explode inside and I couldn't resist any longer. The panties came off! He then was inside me, not all the way because of my request, but enough that tingles flowed through my spine. He was wonderful! Afterwards we just naturally clung to each other talking + giggling. He told me that he found me very attractive – what he would say as the complete package. My appearance combined with my personality and cheerfulness. He said how he wished I would never leave and how we should of known about each other two weeks ago. He gave me three different addresses to reach him – and reminded me continually while taking me home to include a return address in my letter so he could write me back. He is everything I've ever dreamed, wished, or hoped for. I pray that he was sincere in his feelings that he expressed to me. I feel like there was a spark that we clicked mentally and physically – hopefully he felt it too. I have no idea how I am going to face Jason. Daniel treated me the way I was meant to be treated. Jason is a moron – thinking of him right now repulses me I can't imagine him touching me or kissing me. I seriously am going to have to break up with him somehow.

I don't feel guilty – I feel deprived of what I rightfully deserve – to feel like I did all of the time!

Sunday 8/11/96

I never really finished friday's entry. That night James, I , Dave, Paul, and Mike all went out. We went bowling over at the Limerick bowling alley. I came up w/ an 88 and so did Mike – which was weird because he had the hots for me. Anyway, the game was free and all I had to pay for were the shoes – $1.50. Then after that we went to the movies – saw it for free too, Dave had a friend that worked there – it's good to have connections! The movie wasn't that great – but it was free so what the hell! On the way home was the funniest part of the evening. Mike keep trying to get my pants off in the back seat of James car – it was like a scene from a movie – I couldn't stop laughing. A very eventful night – I'll have to give James a call again – I sprained my wrist today – sucked!

Sunday 8/18/96

I've been talking to James B. a lot lately – he's sweet and he listens! I fractured my ocular bone of my wrist – it happened last Sunday and I didn't get a cast until Friday – I fell rollerblading! Go figure! On Thursday I went over Jason's house to see him for the 1st time in 3 weeks – it was nice to see him – but I still had to break up with him – he didn't really react, but I know he will be thinking about me! Also my roommate – Oona – called. She was really nice and I'm pretty sure she is black – I thought I would be real upset but I'm not. She seems very sweet and I'm sure we'll get along fine – I just hope there are no problems because she isn't white! Only about 5 more days! Wow – Ooh I wrote to Daniel, the letter was mailed last Monday – it will be a week tomorrow – I do hope that he'll write me but I am prepared for the fact that he might never respond! Though it did seem that it was meant to be – like when Harry met Sally! Well there are many more adventures awaiting me the next four years – I am ready to take all of them on!

Sunday 8/25/96
Moved into college yesterday! My room is so small. My assumption was correct – Oona is black and a sweetheart – as tiny as she is. Moving in was horrible – everything was so confusing! Then I meet Keira – she's in 203A of my suite– her roomate is a dork – she kind of scares me – that she is a lesbian – her voice is so domineering like a male's – not the tone but the texture. Anyway Keira and I are already the best of buds. Last night we skipped the orientation stuff and got "piss-ass drunk" as Keira puts it. I like her – she is boy crazy just like me! She likes Jamie T. – whom I went to High school with. There are a lot of dorks in the freshman class – all of the really attractive girls – popular - play soccer – hook up w/ the soccer guys. We were all drinking together last night – it was great. I hope Daniel received my letter. I want to tell him all about college and I can't wait to see him again – Ooh I definitely can't wait. I've meet some guys – none really float my boat – I'd rather have Daniel!

Wednesday 8/28/96
So much has happened! On Sunday night and Monday night I got drunk too! Sunday night we (Eileen, Erin, Keira and I) all went out drinking at 702. On Mon night Keira had soccer initiation and was really messed up. I held her head in a bucket while she threw up. She's ok though. Then I went out after she fell asleep and I messed everything up. When I was drunk I told Chris that I really wanted Dan by accident and then Chris told Dan! So then Dan pulled me out in the hallway and said "no, I can't, I have a girlfriend." I felt like crawling into a whole and dying! I can't even apologize to him because I feel weird – I don't know what to do! Also I came back over to Reimert and I was falling all over myself and this guy Alex (a wrestler) held me and took me back to

my room – he was so nice nice – and he acted like he really liked me – then he said Hi to me when I was signing up for office and I said hi back – but nonchalantly and yesterday when I went up to his room to give him a blow–pop he acted as if he didn't even care I was there, and then today when I saw him I waved and smiled, but he just nodded his head and put up his hand – I don't understand Chris was really nice though and walked me home at 2:30am. I wonder if Dan told all the soccer girls what I did – I feel so horrible – now I have a background. Everything is messed up and I miss Kelly! Daniel hasn't even written me! The only really good thing that's happened is that Bobby called – he's a sweetheart! Ooh Kyle – History class

Tuesday 9/3/96
Daniel still hasn't wrote me so tonight I wrote 2 letters to send out. I hope he gets one of them – I would really like to see him again. School is very hard – so much reading. I was drunk again this past weekend. I hooked up w/ this guy Nicholas (*zeta chi*) – big mistake – got a huge purple hickey! I kissed some other guys too (in a card drinking game last week). Made a new friend – little Jewish guy – nice. I'm not going to drink this weekend, my reputation is not as I wish it to be – I didn't have sex w/ anyone but Daniel – how I miss him! People are weird. Nothing feels right – and I stress the word feels. Keira and I will be roommates soon – that's good. I might play lacrosse – I don't feel at home here yet – still in Limbo – there is someone who I found very interesting –a boy named Alex – he seems demented somewhat in a way that borders on the insanity line - whereas insanity is mistaken for genius - because he truly is a genius – by his writing and just his presence. He has become my focus - so hard to read – to comprehend his thoughts – he seems normal when first initiated into his world – but then his walls fade and there is a person with so much depth that they themselves can't even find their thoughts – he is miraculous – never met anyone like him – his mood swings

are very discouraging yet I will be patient and I will endure – this is my mission – I want to find him –not only for my sake but his sake as well.

Saturday 9/21/96

So much has gone by. Joanna is here right now – sleeping. Tonight something weird happened – Scott, who has become a really good friend of mine grabbed my face and kissed me – his girlfriend was right there – but she was turned around and didn't see what happened – Last night I was really drunk - I left a message on Scott's voice mail that I don't even remember doing. I hooked up w/ a boy – Tom – I hope that it wasn't a really bad mistake. He plays football and lives in the suite w/ the popular football freshman boys who both probably know now – at least Joe does because he said something to me at Maples. Tom took my # - wonder if he will call? Daniel hasn't called back yet? It is his turn to write a letter now. Tomorrow there is some kind of lacrosse game that I'm going to. I have poison something all over my left hand – cast came off – and I hope it doesn't keep spreading – really itchy. My life right now is so confusing – so many changes – there are so many things to think about and consider – will Tom call – will I get good grades – meet my future husband – have a good job? Sometimes I just cry – college is very fun but there is always a concern in the back of my head about the future.

Tuesday 9/24/96

Everything is so confusing. School is too much to handle – I got a 45% on my History paper – now I have to redo it. I'm pretty sure the Bobby thing is over with – it's funny how just a couple of months can change someone's perception of others. Scott and his girlfriend broke up – if that, I don't even think they were ever really going out. Tom hasn't called and I don't think he will. Daniel hasn't called or written either. I really want to see him – he is perfect, I don't think I will ever look back on him as a mistake.

When I think about Jason now I am disgusted – I can never see
him again! I was an idiot – how could I put up with the horrible
person that he is – and to think I picked him out as what I wanted,
how horrible the male choices at Bear High must have been. I feel
overwhelmed with work and with social structures here. I'm sick
of the get drunk weekend partying – I want a person (guy) to hang
out with, someone to talk to and listen. I miss Kelly – she always
listened to me – always made everything seem less important in
the scheme of things. I seem to be crying a lot – maybe that is a
reaction to stress. Things aren't really going according to my
plans. I need stability and there is none – Daniel is something to
me that I never had before and I don't really know how to feel or
what to do – I know that I want to see him but will that make my
feelings for him stronger, and then when he goes back will I feel
alone even more? I need to stop worrying about men – concentrate
on myself – that is what I'm here for – to educate myself. I know a
lot of people but there is no one I can really talk to who will
understand exactly how I feel and then know what to do for me.
All I do is worry + study. I have no time for myself – no time to
be free in a sense – to do things that energize my thoughts – to
even contemplate over occurrences. I am not smart, athletic, or
popular here. I think that there is something very essential to my
life that is either lacking or missing. What it is I don't really know
yet.

Wednesday 10/2/96
I'm feeling better. I've become much better friends w/ the soccer
girls; Tara, Samantha, and Laura seemed to really click w/ me –
Karen and I really don't talk much but she is nice to me. I called
Daniel on Thursday night – I loved talking to him. We talked
about how he is a rationalist and I'm an idealist – psych stuff.
How it was fate that we met again and how everything worked out.
He told me how he loved that I was tall and I asked him why and
he said "when I look at you it's just like WOW!" – wow! Then I

just got a letter from him on Monday w/ a picture – he looks kind of weird in his picture but he is still sooo cute! Also on Sat when I was drunk my friend Adam from Demas asked me to go to his fraternity formal with him – so today I had to go out and buy a dress. Adam is really nice and we've been friends since the beginning of the year – but when I asked him why he asked me to the formal he said cause "I like you a real lot"? Nah – I hope he doesn't try to "make a move" or anything because I will feel so stupid – I don't like him in that way. I mean he is good looking + tall but not of my taste. I want to write Daniel + tell him all about it but I never have time. Last night was really fun – Alex, Scott, and I were wrestling. Alex who is an actual wrestler was kind of teaching me/beating the crap out of me – needless to say I never pinned either of them but they sure pinned me, but I never gave up – always fought until the end. I love them both, they're like the brothers I never had – I even annoy them like a little sister! They don't even think of me as a girl – I love it – I can be a big fat pig + belch right in front of them!

Tuesday 10/15/96

I was so drunk after the fraternity homecoming formal – I could hardly walk and when I got back to my room Keira started yelling at me – I couldn't take it, she made me get so depressed – I tried to slit my wrists. Scott caught me, he was really upset and scared – he told me he would miss me and I think he said I love you – Alex was pretty freaked out too. I guess they care about me – though they don't show it sometimes. Scott has another girlfriend now – I hate when he has a girlfriend, I feel weird when I'm around them both. Joanna visited on Sunday, then Kelly last night. Things are all right with the History Paper due on Friday – Aaah – I wrote Daniel about my family – my mom, I hope it doesn't freak him out. Then I sent him a map to get here and a T-shirt. Can't wait to see him!

At the homecoming formal this 28 year old guy was talking to me. He was in a different section at a bar and stopped me when I walked out of the bathroom to talk and I can't get him out of my head! He told me he liked my black mini cocktail dress and he asked me how old I was. His eyes got so big when I told him I was 18, he was like "how are you at the bar?" and I told him I was there for the fraternity formal in the banquet room. Then he grabbed my shoulders and pushed me against the hallway wall and started kissing me so intensely, he wanted me to leave with him. He pressed himself against me so hard that I couldn't move and he put both his hands on my thighs up under my dress. He was so intense, he wanted me to leave with him and never go back to school. He said that I didn't need to go to college and that he would take care of me forever. I really wanted to leave with him and never come back but I wasn't sure if he was a serial killer or not – I thought about him all night after. Adam caught us together near the bathrooms after I was missing for a while and he started screaming at me. Even when my date showed up the 28 year old still was like come with me right now to my car and he was pulling my hand. He was so powerful and I didn't know what to do? Adam, my date, started flipping out on him to leave me alone and they started fighting. It was really nuts! Then Adam was so mad at me for kissing the stranger that he made me sit alone on the bus ride home and screamed at me from the back the whole ride since I ruined his senior homecoming formal (excerpt from "Dream Secrets").

Wednesday 10/23/96
Daniel's supposed to visit tomorrow. I feel so ugly – so, so, so ugly. There are so many things wrong with me – he doesn't even know. When he realizes all the faults what will he do? I cannot deal w/ this – I don't know him well enough to share my faults that I cannot hide – I hate my skin – it is so messed up – why me – why can't I just have normal skin – I have to do so much just to <u>feel</u>

presentable. Why am I being punished. I don't even like it, how can anyone else! I cannot deal w/ this – I'm not ready - -I'm not comfortable w/ him. All I can do is cry. I feel so horribly ugly.

Saturday 10/26/96
Daniel came, he didn't look the same as he looked at the shore when he was a lifeguard – he looked more serious and more nerdy. I don't know what happened but his nose looked like someone broke it. He is really nice + caring. I just don't know if I was attracted to him – his sweetness makes up for it. We talked a lot and I told him that we should be friends – to start over kind of in a basic way. We did kind of have sex – or at least tried on both nights – I had to pee, then he felt bad on the second – because of how we were talking. Samantha + Laura said that he was a gentleman and he is. He's very serious though. He opened up to me and told about his mother's alcoholism, how it affected his life last winter. He's my friend for life – I know it. Now I feel like I have nothing to look forward to, no one to think about. I'm o.k.. – I'm really glad that we talked about the 1st time (Aug) and know how we feel.

Sunday 10/27/96
The clock says 5:00am. Tonight was Tara's B-Day party. I had 4 shots of vodka and some beers! Keira got drunk and told me that she hated Daniel and that he was a fuckin' asshole! What a bitch – then she said that she was mad at me. I did feel bad – but she totally agreed to him coming up – fuckin' bitch – I don't want to be her roommate anyway. I went over to talk to James – stupid bitch likes him – I asked him if he liked her, and not only did he not like her, he thought she was not attractive, I knew it. I feel asleep in Andrew's bed – I wanted to, always thought he was cute. Boy do I have a headache anyway. We hooked up – I shouldn't of – oh well. The best part is the football boys and I were all talking, James is so cool – we're friends now - I put a big goose-egg on his

fore-head poor guy - I had him in a headlock and slipped and fell against the wall and slammed his head – poor guy – I felt so bad, I held his head in my lap and then scratched his back to help him fall asleep. Oh God that would ruin everything 'cause we were in Killer's bed – I know he would hate me – Please, I hope I didn't. I left my shoes their (on purpose) I'll get them later.

Thursday 10/31/96
Halloween – Booh!   Last night I went out w/ Scott, Cecile, Alex, and that dork Bret mischiefing – we had eggs – I never really got to use mine. It was funny! Andrew says high to me whenever he see's me – so does everyone in 304 – love the 304 football boys forever! Killer (heart) even told me that he put my shoes in the common room for me to get – awesome. I'm glad they are nice – It's all good with them. I'm feeling better. Wonder if Daniel has written me yet? Killer was a second away from egging me in the face! He said" you're lucky Mary" and I was thinking – you are so hot – come sweep me off my feet you idiot! So many boys – I must be good – no more hook ups – GOOD GOOD IS WHAT I AM!

Tuesday 11/19/96
Well I did call Bobby – it was nice, I called Daniel last night – talked for over two hours – he slept with someone else a few weeks ago – girl he dated in high school, best friend type-serious relationship – not really sure how I feel about that. It was nice to talk to him especially since no one here gives a damn – maybe Laura to an extent. I don't have any close friends – I really realize that and it's scary – I have to call people and e-mail people to even feel like a real person. I want to transfer somewhere else. No one is my friend – they are all Keira's and just to prove my point – Laura + Stacia came up and I was walking into my room and I said – what are you guys doing – oh coming to visit you and they

didn't even bother to come in as soon as they realized that Keira wasn't here!

Monday 12/9/96

Thanksgiving wasn't very good! I was sick with a fever of 103 – Joanna and I only spent Friday night together – and my younger cousin came along for a little while. I have been pretty depressed lately – not very happy with my appearance – I look like crap – skin is all fucked up. I spent the last week or two confined to my self – alone, not spending any time with anyone. Jeremy – my manager at Pop's has asked for my phone # - Eric the other manager saw me in Boot Girl at Zerns and told me to call him at work later – so I did and gave him my school # for Jeremy – he had better give me a ring! O.k.. that was the beginning of good things. Spent the weekend at home! Today has been good in general. Michael from high school has been writing me e-mail everyday – he is always there for me and I am glad that he is my friend. Ooh Daniel's B-day was on Dec 4th – I was a weakling and gave him a call – I felt neither happy nor sad after the brief conversation so I am not sure what that means – but I don't think about him much anymore at all. I had my very last History class today and I am so happy about that. I also had to pass out papers in psych class as a favor to my new advisor – that was a new experience having everyone kind of stare at me. Staring boy (in POD) – he hasn't been staring recently – the whole 1st two months of school he was always looking at me and now all the sudden he stopped, and I never really noticed him at much first then when I did notice him he stopped staring which I miss greatly and now I sort of want him + he is pretty short but I don't even care I still want him. I haven't been spending much time w/ Scott at all. Tonight I was feeling pretty good about myself so I went up – he was really nice and we hung out for a while – then I went with Cecile to go pick up some sandwiches at Bravo's pizza. When we came back I stayed for a while then left. I went to do e-mail and then I visited Laura – I really like her she is so nice and sweet and easy to talk to! I spent about 2 hours in her room talking. Her and Samantha are definitely my favorite friends here. My roommate Keira is never even here anyway, she hardly ever even sleeps in here – she is always up in Samantha's suite talking and stuff – NEVER here! Is she avoiding me – who knows – who cares at this point anyway it is like I have a single! Back to staring boy – well I e-mailed him a little message like a big dork! I am such a tard. He better e-mail me back – I will feel so stupid if he doesn't. After I left Laura's I went to Samantha's suite and then over to Scott. We got into this huge pillow fight which he started – and he beat the living shit out of my head – I just was not in sink – I couldn't hit him, but he keep pounding me like an idiot. I wouldn't give up even though he told me I should then I fell down – almost passing out, he literally picked me up and took me outside though I was still ready to fight and I forgot I stopped by Heather's earlier to talk – I'll talk with her more later!

Thursday 12/19/96
Drank too much of vodka on the 10th – 10 shots in 30 minutes? Walked over to Curtis – yelling for staring boy – was written up I had to see Takita. Wrote staring boy an email and he found out about me looking for him – he called me – we talked for a while – ended weird though he never called back when he said he would after 5 minutes. Keira saw him in the library the next day - she told him "Listen you don't understand Mary, you can either be there for her or you can't, there is no in between – because you will just confuse her" – I think that's the best thing she has ever done for me – I like that she said that – show's that she cares about my feelings. Staring boy emailed me the next day to say hi and to talk later – I guess that means he wants to be there. Jeremy, my manager at Pop's Restaurant, called me on Sunday – I never got a chance to call him back until Tuesday - busy with finals. He wasn't home – I went to work today, it was pretty fun. Jeremy

wasn't there though. There is an employee x-mas party on Tue from 2-4 so I think I will go to that – Jeremy and I will be working together that that might be the first time I see him – I have this awesome outfit I want to wear – red Q pants – tank top – slick baby slick!

Daniel – I don't think much of him anymore at all. He is hard to even explain – my feelings for him that is. There really aren't any – which is kind of bad for me. When I was leaving – this guy Beau – one who called me in the beginning of the semester said bye to me –gave me a big hug – he is the only one, all my friends went to dinner and didn't bother with me – tards!! He always calls me sweetheart or babe - or some chauvinistic name – I kind of like the attention.

I never said bye to Scott – he basically treats me like a princess half the time and then like crap the other half I am very displeased with him and his attitude. We fight and he just gets way to violent. I am ok with all my friends at school but happy to see Joanna and Kelly. The only thing I want for x-mas is to have a boy – Jeremy – to cuddle with and spend time – he better get his act together and call me.

Friday 12/27/96
Christmas sucked! My mother, Robin, didn't even bother to buy me anything – she gave me a $50 bill today – I'll put it towards the stereo I will buy – finally a CD player. My cousins left today – I don't like them at all – prissy heaven!!! I know what I want my new year resolution to be – not to bother myself with worrying about guys so much! My whole diary is about guys – my whole life revolves around guys. I went rollerblading today for the first time in 6 months – tightened my wheels finally. Went to work from 4-7:30. Jeremy said hi to me – thought nothing of it, we were just like acquaintances - so I figured o.k. no sweat – and spent

most of the time talking to Nick – which I didn't realize would create a problem later. When I left Nick kind of suggested that he and I should get together "sometime " – "what are you doing tonight - nothing – "Gee if I got off work earlier then we could hang out" – ooh? So then I said bye to everyone and left I was putting the key into my car door – drove the convertible – and I noticed Jeremy's car one spot away and he usually parks over with everyone else – but being non-excited over guys anymore – I didn't think anything of it – I still kept that mind state even when I looked over and saw him running out of Pop's towards me and his car of course. I asked what he had forgotten and then he said he wanted a smoke and then he proceeded to apologize for his actions at the Christmas party (basically ignored me) and that night (same as before). He needed my # - I gave it to him – I was utterly surprised I had come to my own conclusion that he wasn't even faintly interested. Wow – he thought that whole thing out – parked the car next to mine – patienced himself to come out at the right time – thought it was a bit odd at first, unless people usually run to their car for cigarettes!! I have considered writing a book after I filled the pages of this diary – I think it would be a good idea, though I really don't want everyone to know my personal feelings and actions of about 2 whole – very important – years of my life – the transition from high school to college, girl to woman, adolescent to adult. Maybe I would change names or something so no one would know it was me who wrote it!

Wednesday 1/1/97
All I can do is weep! Aaaahh I hate him – I hate my father. I hate my life, I am worthless my life is meaningless, I should have died when I was 5 months old. I have no destiny – I should have died – no respect, all I feel, all the time is pain.

Tuesday 1/7/97

I am haunted by the desire for the love found in romance novels.
A long lost loved revived over years of separation, rekindled to last
an eternity. "The Notebook" which I read tonight shallows my
world to that I have never found love and frightens me too that I
never will. The person who I most think about is Scott – he
resembles the closes to what I desire in his care for me and
feelings, though I could never evolve anything from us now due to
that he is too immature in his youth and would spoil the feelings I
have grown to endure for him. I dream a fantasy in 4 years he will
realize his love for me and before we graduate from college he will
decide that we were meant to be and will then be together. Do I
have a destiny, Justin, a forever lust from high school has been
reintroduced into my life through a meaningless part-time job. He
mentioned my working there to forever friend and neighbor Kelly.
What can come of this? What can come of anything? My lost
innocence past and forgotten, and a new well defined desire for
what I have always yearned – a true love, kind and inspiring.
When I fall in love it will be forever and I will know it. I can
easily perceive my future – meeting a nice guy, kind, and a good
man, becoming engaged and then knowing. Knowing that I can't
spend the rest of my life knowing that the man I married isn't my
soul mate, the love is there but it isn't true, it is missing the magic
that pours from the romance novels that dreams are built upon. I
am a dreamer, a romantic and I won't settle until I find him. He
must be out there, he must exist, and I will search everlastingly for
my destiny.

Thursday 1/16/97

Working at Pop's Restaurant has been a wonder. Old Justin works
there now! On Wednesday Nick, Jeremy, Justin and I worked – it
was hilarious. Justin + Jeremy even got me to try some pot –
didn't really do anything – going to do something on Friday. I
wrote a bunch of things about my "friends" at college in the book I

was reading. I'll have to recopy into this sometime (see below) – today Oprah said that people should write down 5 things a day that they are thankful for – I don't think I could do it. – Justin at work acts strange – not so much making jokes about me, but saying and acting as though he likes me or something? Remember – men are not important – just be friends!!!! New Year – fresh start. I guess I am happy – don't want to go back to school – don't like my "friends" – don't like much of anyone!

Friends floating on the surface of the ocean of thought, whereas I have sunk into the depth of the water searching for answers and contemplating what the future will bring. When there is nothing to analyze or depict in my surrounding environment I become bored and then must, therefore, entertain myself with my overdeveloped sense of humor and silly actions, which then in turn may lead to me appearing trivalent and blatantly "stupid" or "dumb" which are only the mere appearance of my own self entertainment. The appearance of such connotative action leads people to underestimate my intelligence leading to very forthright actions and speech since they do not realize my capability and depth of thought. I am a loner; people do not evoke my thought often, but it comes from within my own world. If I had to live constantly with surrounding people I would most definitely become neurotic ad unable to function. I believe that I am changing before my very eyes, not physically of course, yet, emotionally with the advent of my new year resolution. I will not let the strive for men or love or whatever run my life – I want to strive for my own success and be my own person in need of no one for security. I want so much to do this easy thought, yet I find it so difficult! My mind often wonders to thoughts of Scott and how he has done such things to reveal to mean of his caring heart. What I am determined to maintain is the power I control over the mystery of who I am to onlookers. I have lost that power to many too soon as college began and I will not do so any further! I will be unknowing and unattainable to all eyes that wonder over me. I will have power again revived. I will not be a slave to lust, yet become what is lusted for. I will concentrate on my studies and develop my inner thoughts. I will read books and know all I yearn to know. Everyone says that "these years are the best years of your life – so enjoy them" have either never went to college or did and was one of those people who could only float upon the ocean of thought. Life would be simple if you never have to think about things – (what) my friends have accomplished so well. Not to say they don't think, of course they think, just not profound thoughts on life. Joanna and Kelly have had deep discussions with me on political, social, religious, and other issues which I have (yet) to experience with my college buddies. I announced to them that I had read a full book in one sitting and they responded "that seems pretty dorkish Mare." If they only knew how I despised being their friend at that moment because of their only being frivolous gossip and getting the guy. None of them open up to me of any depth of thought, about guys – yes, not about worldly concerns or inner questions. I don't think I will ever fit in anywhere. I am adored for the reason that people consider me funny and humorous – due to the appearance of my own entertainment – but I do not want to be known for such with the "air-headish" depiction not far behind. I want to be admired for how I think and the strong emotions that I feel, that are considered by my friends to be an annoyance, which churns my hatred for them more. I do think I am changing, not to have such unimportant actions take place to relish at my soul and corrupt my reputation. I have regained much more composure than I had begun with and I should then keep building as the second semester starts.

Saturday 1/18/97
Yesterday night I went out with Kelly, Angie, Jeremy, and Justin (also Rob and Josh showed up later). We went and played pool – I did alright. Then we went back to their place. This was the first

night I really "smoked up" – it didn't seem to affect me very much, but Jeremy said that it did – of course Robin managed to ruin the evening (I called to say that I was going to be late coming home and she *69'ed back and demanded that they send me home or she was going to call the police!) – Jeremy called today to make sure I was alright. I like the fact that he was even somewhat concerned. Tonight I returned to Knoll, for yet another dance, which I thought I would never do again! Bobby was nowhere to be found I saw Jeremy at the end, we talked for a while and he gave me his # and I would definitely like to call him sometime! I had done something I never did before – I asked some guy to dance – Alex – he was looking at me a lot and he seemed quiet and nice so I figured why not – who cares what anyone thinks, and who am I to judge people, he could turn into a great friend. I am going to miss the people from Pop's. I hope they keep in touch. I am not looking forward to going back to school. I don't think that is a good sign. My neighbors the Beyer's gave me a church speech tonight – I couldn't escape. What a weekend!

Tuesday 1/28/97

This past weekend was a blur – drinking Thur – Sat. Went against my promise and hooked up with staring boy – stupid me, ended up just like all the others. Been going over to Jeremy's townhouse – was over Sat. night – was trashed – he rubbed my feet again, he is so sweet – I do think I like him – hope it doesn't backfire in my face. My "friends" all suck and were treating me bad as usual so I went down to the tau sig suite. They were all very nice to me and gave me good advice – this Erica girl who is a senior told me a story about how she was harassed and hated living here – she's nice! I do need new friends – this is a bunch of bullshit!! I think I am becoming stronger as a person, which is good. Got a sorority bid from tau sig yesterday. I'll probably pledge there, rush was fun on Fri!

Tuesday 2/4/97

Ooh – I start pledging tau sig on Fri – 3 weeks of hell! Lacrosse started yesterday – very very sore, 6:30am practices! Jeremy is still around – he came over Saturday night and we stayed in my room for a while and talked. Friday was fun – to the dated I wore my leopard outfit – was very trashed – danced w/ everyone - the D.J.'s – Andy + Joe. Very very busy I am going to die this next month!

Monday 2/10/96

Weekend – literally one hour of sleep – pledging rough – today was fun though.

Wednesday 3/5/97

Pledging is finally over – it was rough – I love my sisters though, except for that one girl of course – no one loves her! Last night I got drunk – I love Scott - don't even know what to do. He doesn't even realize – moron! I went and hung out w/ Shane (POD) – got very high w/ him, Mike, and this other guy Dave. Hmmm – Jason from high school emailed me a couple of times, so did Josh (who sat at my high school prom table) - he sent me a virtual postcard for Valentine's day. Haven't <u>talked</u> to Jeremy in 3 weeks because of pledging – oh well. Keira and I are getting along so well – I am very glad – like we did in the beginning of the year – we're buds again – and also 305 girls, everything is great. Oh I made friends with this guy Mike – I was looking for him last night – NOT sure why – people found out and think I was stalking him or something – whatever! Kelly is with Nick from Pop's now – I am really happy for her! I talked to Bobby the other night – he doesn't seem too interested, maybe because I was not very interested in kissing him when we met up at the park near my college – that's o.k., I don't care. Boys don't really matter, my friendships are what matters! I don't have a relationship w/ anyone because I just compare them to Scott – I hate him and love him at the same time.

I hate him because he doesn't realize and I know we will never end up together and I love him because I think he is so the first guy that really cares and worries for me, that he has said he loved me. My feelings for him keep getting stronger and stronger – I need to separate myself from him, maybe I can forget about him. I am saddened to think of the future – him and his wife and me seeing him at reunions.

Monday 3/24/97
Sat night went to the Wings lacrosse game – was so drunk, it was so much fun – Melissa and Jackie came back and hung out in 302! K was there, and Brian from abnormal psych class, they all knew me and remembered things from the beginning of the year. I haven't been going up to Scott's room at all. I am testing him to see if he really is my friend and cares for me then he will eventually miss me and come to me, instead of me always going to him. Saw Joanna on Friday. She is really going to go to Lehigh next year. Jeremy has been done with for a while, ever since after pledging (could not talk to him for three weeks, no boys allowed during pledging, thanks sorority). I don't really know what I want to do now. Guys – smuys. Lacrosse is alright – I guess, she puts me into the LOOSER group. I'd better start practicing harder, this will not be good for my image.

Monday 4/21/97
Everything is just out of control – my grades are fine, but it's just my impulses, I can't control them at all. I had hooked up w/ this boy Derik and then I hooked up with three guys in one night – was naked w/ one, and naked from the bottom down w/ the other two – Judd (APE) and Marco – Marco and I had sex – don't know what I was thinking or if I wanted to? – then Derik (POD) – he was the one I was naked naked with. I almost had sex with two of these boys in the same night and I did have sex with another one! Well APEs fraternity found out about everything and would not let it go.

Judd came over again – he slept over on the Thursday after (sex on April 5th + hook ups, and Judd slept over on the 10th) – I didn't even have any makeup on, and he spent the entire night – two firsts to never have occurred before? Judd did some pretty <u>nice</u> things for me that night, but I wouldn't have sex with him – ah ha!! I am 19 now – pretty old, that's the same age Daniel was when I meet him, he was 19 and I was 17, now he is 21 and I am 19, boy how so much can change in two years. I am scared to think of where I will be two years from now. I really need to stop my crying – I get way too upset so easily, I have to go to counseling now because I kept threatening to kill myself around people when I was drunk. Also I don't know why I am being so crazy with the boys. I am on the pill now so maybe that could be affecting me. I really like Scott and Alex, they have been being pretty decent to me – even treating me like a real friend. Alex has been weird, he looks at me as if he is just not looking at me, but he is looking at me with more than just his eyes, like he is feeling something more behind what he shows and I can see it in his eyes! – they are the windows to your soul you know!!!! My sorority formal is on Sat., I am going with this senior Steve – really great guy from what I have seen of him. Wonder if I will hook up with him. Probably? Why in the world am I being so impulsive and so very sexual??? I don't want to be portrayed like this! Urgh – oh well, I will be dead some day and none of this will even matter.

Saturday 5/10'97
School is pretty much over for me. I have moved all of my things home. I just have two finals on Monday and that is it. I wanted to come home this weekend because I really don't want to be there. On Tuesday, the last day of classes, all of us were hangin' out in Samantha's room. I was drinking rum and coke – a lot. Then we all went over to Omach – APO's house and I was looking for a beer, and Henry (a senior) saw me and said that he had beer in his room – so I followed him into his room. It was no big deal – we

were friends and we were just sitting in there, talking – I can't even remember what about. He locked the door and came over to where I was sitting and sat down next to me. He kissed me and then one thing led to another. Being drunk isn't an excuse, I know that, but I did not, in anyway, intend for that to happen. We were friends and I don't know why it happened and I know that doing things like this are so morally wrong and what people might think of me if they ever found out (now I have had sex with two guys since my first Daniel for a total of three!). He is a wrestler and was so aggressive and so strong and his skin was so soft and kisses so gentle and the combination of those things was just too much for me in my drunken state. I must say now that I cannot drink anymore – for a long time. I don't want to be the crazy nymph of the campus. I want to fall in love, and I want to be in love, and I want to make love! What in the world am I doing – this is so wrong. I told Scott and Alex what happened. They know that this isn't right for me. Wednesday night I must of spent 3 or 4 hours talking to them. If they only knew how I love both of them with all my heart and that I am so sad because next year we will all be separated. If they only knew I truly love them both and I don't love guys – I never do – but I love them. Why can't I find someone to love so I can get away from those things that I am doing.

Tuesday 5/27/97
Hmmm, Daniel – not good thoughts! Don't really care though …. I now have a problem that I never had to deal with though American women have - I am getting FAT!!! I really am and I hate it. I don't have self control about anything. I need to run!!! I applied for a second job at the Pottstown Diner, working around food is not good for me. I have to plan – I want to work as a waitress over the summer and then when school starts I want to work at Harpoon Louie's and keep busy. Work out in the Gym and just do everything for myself. Everything for me!! No parties

– No stupid boys – nothing. Work – Exercise – Study – sounds good. No time for any socializing – I need to work on myself and realize who I am for a while! I don't really like anyone at college anyway – I won't miss anyone.

Sunday 6/1/97
This past weekend was the prom. Kelly went with Nick. I went and rented a motel room for them for after the prom. Well she's not in the V club anymore, she lost it on her prom night – how fairy tale like! I am happy for her and now I have someone to talk to. Kelly, Kristen and Joanna are my best friends and I think they will be for years to come.

Sunday 6/8/97
I started working at the Limerick Diner as a waitress – money is good, made a new friend Tim goes to Swathmore College. Worked with Matt H. tonight, he's strange and I can't figure him out. I have no boys to lust after!!!! – very lonely when there is just you. I need something to hope for or else I am so bored. I am upset that I am upset about not having a boy. I need some excitement!

Sunday 6/29/97
Lucas??? He has been around here lately. One night I went to the YMCA and worked out with him and his friend Jay. Afterwards we went swimming in Jay's pool and then in the Jacuzzi (in our B-day suits Ha Ha) – it was fun. I don't want them to start liking me or anything, because then it would be weird! Joanna and I bought tickets to the Rage Against the Machine concert in Camden, NJ – it is going to be wild, we'll be killed but oh well – it's going to be the BEST!! Bob had heart surgery – he is OK now. I have no one to like – this is weird. Kelly, Kristen, Joanna and I are supposed to go to Dorney Park sometime soon – love roller coasters! I had to

wait on Rick and Dan from high school the other night at Limerick Diner. Urgh!

Thursday 7/3/97
Blah – Blah – everything is just blah, I hate where I work, I don't want any friends – I just hate everything. My grandfather might die – then everything will just be horrible. Why can't I change! AAAAHHH I am home – all alone – grandma took Bob to the hospital – nothing to do, seems to be the story of my life.

Saturday 7/19/97
Life is going by so fast – my weekends disappear due to work and my weeks just fly by in a daze of afternoons with the neighbors and Joanna. Only about a month until college starts – urgh. I still am not sure what to do about Lucas – I do care for him, yet I am not sure in what way I care for him? I guess time will tell. He called today, though I wasn't home – I won't see him for 2 weeks now.

Tuesday 7/22/97
Yesterday night was hysterical. Joanna, Kristen, and I were cruising around in the woody. Joanna was driving because I was still a little drunk – I passed out in Kristen's room earlier. We drove all over and Kristen and I were standing up – Jason passed us – ha ha. Then we went over to Jeremy's house and left a shopping cart with trash in it on their step. Then I grabbed this huge tree branch from the road and a broom and mop which we left on the Beyers porch – ha ha. It was so fun to be vandals! I still think about Lucas a lot – whatever should I do – I guess nothing right now – oh well. I'll just let happen what will happen.

Tuesday 8/5/97
This past week and a half has been quite active, probably the most this summer. Last Monday, a week ago, Lucas called – we talked for a while and then it happened. We planned for him to sneak

over through the basement after everyone was sleep – all was successful – I was his first kiss plus more! On Tuesday night – the next day, Kristen slept over. I left the garage door open and the keys in the convertible. At around 3:00 am we got dressed in our robber attire and proceeded out through the basement. We push the car out of the garage and started it up down the street. We put pads all over Jeremy's front door and on the table in back of the house. It was very fun – I admit. When Kristen and I came home there was a little problem, the car stopped right in front of her house. Kristen steered the car while I pushed it to the house. After a lot of effort, we finally got the car in the garage and snuck back into the house – mission completed! On Friday I went to work as usually and when I came home something unexpected happened. I pulled into the garage and when I got out of the car Lucas was there in the driveway. It would have been a romantic notion, expect he startled me into a frantic scream! I guess he remembered that my grandparents were away that weekend. I had secretly hoped that he would come over because I never got the chance to ask him. I was pleasantly surprised after the initial frighteness. We played some more, but now I am fearful that I am using him just for fun – I must reconsider our relations. The next night, Saturday, Timmy from work had invited me to a "get-together" at his friend's house! I went and had a few Rolling Rocks + a shot of gin – needless to say – I was drunk. It was nice though – we talked. I fell asleep and was awoken to the sound of Timmy throwing up all over himself in his sleep on the chair across from me – what am image to remember. Then I left, it was around 5:00 am. I made use of the weekend because it is a rare event to have no one home expect me! Last night Kristen slept over and we were "sipping some juice" – had fun – did body art and took pictures!

Thursday 8/21/97

Last Saturday was the Rage concert! I loved it – though there were some problems – 1) I thought I left the ticket in the car and Grandma + Bob went to the Pocono's 2) We were jammed on the highway for about 40 minutes 3) we were running out of Gas 4) after the concert we didn't have the key to open the car because Joanna took it off the key chain to open the glove compartment earlier. Everything worked out alright. I saw Angelo – he's nice. Sunday morning I awoke to a phone call from Lucas. I hadn't seen or talked to him in about 2 weeks. He came over and we kidded around. He taught me some football things. I had to go to see the counselor at school to make sure I could register. That was somewhat difficult. Joanna left for Lehigh today – I love her dearly! Hope she does alright. School is starting soon – Ooh great – well "this will be."

Sunday 8/31/97

So college has begun once again. This weekend was so fun – Friday was hysterical, we all got drunk and were partying in the POD suite. Laura and I were bustin' our moves. Saturday night Joanna came up and we had a ball. We both were so drunk and went to the APEs suite. We were falling all over ourselves and the floor, Joanna kissed another boy – her second – Brent then Jim. I ended up with this kid Neil, with whom I had much fun!! – Pooter munchin' – the number was accomplished also! Then today Joanna and I went out to Panda Heaven for Lunch – Yummy. She really is my best friend – I love her dearly! When we're together we cannot – not have fun – it is just impossible – she walked in on us w/ two guys – ah haha!!

Tuesday 9/16/97

Ends up that Neil has a girlfriend – hey there's always something! – things are pretty good. Joanna and I went to Panda Heaven on Friday and I stayed over at my house. Lacrosse practice for fall

ball had started – yesterday. I got a job at the Collegeville Inn.
There are no boys in my life right now – it seems that I just don't
have the time to even think about them. Hopefully one will find
me!

Friday 9/26/97
Kristen came up on Sat. night because I sprained my ankle in a
drunken frenzy. We were bored – didn't want to drink – so we
smoked up – it was horrible because we were sure it was laced. I
was on the gravitron for 3 hours, I was so heavy and couldn't move
or talk. When it first hit me – it was the most wonderful sensation
– better than ever being drunk. But about after 10 seconds I was
scared because I felt that I had no control over myself at all – I
didn't know what I was going to do next. I saw my hand go
through Kristen's body. I was afraid the feeling was never going
to go away. I thought that I might die because my heart was
beating so slow – everything was so slow. Kristen saw the room
spin – it made her sick, and she said her heart was beating faster
than ever. Now that I think about it, I want to do it again, it was
such a strong feeling, now I know it will go away. I am going
home this weekend – I'm bored!

Monday 11/3/97
Homecoming was great! I went to APE's formal with Vince –
despite what my roomate would think. I had a great time – 15
shots and 3 mixed drinks. Jake was being very friendly towards
me. I knew that this had been building since the moment we met.
That night we ended up together – even though he had a girlfriend
– for 3 years no less. In Olin on the floor, on the table,
everywhere. Total nakedness, all bared, yet everything stayed
playfull not serious. I think that it shouldn't have happened, yet it
was inevitable. I told Kelly, Joanna, and Kristen, and then later I
told Scott and Samantha. Until today he made no response to me,
and then today he punched me in the shoulder and said "hey," I

suppose that is good, I hope we can be friends. Though it is weird to me not telling anyone about what happened. I usually rely on the support of other females – especially in the house, to give me advice.

I have been working hard in school – also running and lifting 3 times a week, I feel pretty good about myself. Everyone thinks I have only hooked up with one guy this year – that is good. I think I should be more secretive with my actions and feelings. In a way I am feeling very smart – really – very accomplished. I have a minor now – women's studies – I think I will enjoy it.

This past weekend was Halloween. Kristen slept over at home. We went out Sat. and ran into – Matt H. – was a kick, We went over to his house. I still have a tingle in my bones for him. We really hit it off, and this is why I don't understand his not calling. He might still – I hope he does – because I would like someone off campus that is my "get away" person. I still love Joanna, Kelly, and Kristen dearly. I know we will be friends for life.

Saturday 11/15/97

Sitting in the closet crying – not healthy. I don't understand? I really don't. I should have had someone to care about me by now, I am so stupid. Dumb Jake and Titkas were my dated dates – guess they couldn't find me a real date – the looser that I am. I admit – it was fun, in the beginning, but at the end when everyone had someone I didn't have anyone – how ironic – I start with two dates and end up with none.

I keep thinking about dumb Scott – I can't stop – I want to so bad, I feel like I should be in AA or something like that about him. I need some kind of resolution?

I am not happy at all – Laura is a tard – she doesn't know how to deal with anything. If I blow things out of proportion, then it is my business – she shouldn't become involved. I think I'm going to call Kelly now – hope she is there.

Saturday 11/29/97

Thanksgiving was alright. My cousin came up and the Hunton's were over. Robin was annoying as usual – I feel that I don't even want to be around her. I went to a temp agency so I will have a job over summer, what am I talking about – I mean break – nothin' new!

Thursday 12/18/97

December flew by, how can it already be half over. Finals were rough! I need a boy – Damon – cute freshman wrestler. We talked forever and then he slept over – only minimal activity though, which was very nice. I loved being with him, we had so much in common and listened to Sarah McLachlan all night. Though he turned out to be a jerk which led me then to sleep over at my comforts room, Scott. Him and Sara finally broke up, but now he is with this freshman Brandi – When is he going to get a clue?? I am home now for Christmas – yay, now I can listen to fighting all the time. Another weird event – I can't stop thinking about Neil – He is stuck in my thoughts. I think I am intrigued by the way he always stares at me. I really just want to hate him but I can't and I don't know what to do so I ignore him. I guess there really is a thin line between love and hate. There is some weird connection between us that doesn't seem to go away. I have this overwhelming urge to be with him – I don't know what to do?

Monday 1/5/98

A new year has begun. After school had finished for the semester Annie had a formal get-together at her house. Laura drove to my house and we went to Annie's in so-so weather. Her house was of little excitement. After only 2 hours we then drove to Stacia's house. Her parents (mother) was away and they had gotten a keg. We were of rare form – as usual, with the help of the delightful jello shots. I drove Laura's car home the next morning. (the party was on the 27th after my relatives had left). For new years I went to Laura's house and with her four friends we all ventured to a frat party at Dragon University. The house was as cold as Antarctica in the winter. Laura was totally gone, talking a foreign language at that. The others were also in not so good condition; I was not bad at all. To ring in the new year I had a fling – Jarred was his name. I found him somewhat intriguing for whatever reason. He said that my face was soft, not my skin, yet my face structure itself. I found that sweet, it wasn't a line, just a gesture. I hold him in good regards, he was kind and pleasant! We all drove home the next morning not feeling so good and very groggy, especially the language wonder – Laura!

Laura and I made a new year's resolution that we are not to have anymore "random" hook-ups, for lack of a better term. Though I think it will only apply to Brynell and not when we are on vacation, as to we are going to Dragon University on Friday – you never know what may happen. In consideration, I will never see these people again – all is well!

Saturday 2/7/98
Well – Neil did come and try to talk to me one night at a party – we say hi to each other sometimes – but that's about all. Lacrosse has started – the first week of running practice was hell – 4 miles of sprinting – Now 5:30am morning practices are just great – ya right!!!!

Boys are tards. I have a definite violent tendency towards them – of which they know – They fear me and others say that this is not good – yet I thrive off of it! I believe I am rising up – people are viewing me differently – I am more sought out – I have connections – therefore power, which all want to have. I will accomplish my college goal.

Pledging has begun for the freshman. 3 girls dropped at 1:30am on the 1st night. That's a fuckin' joke – they are PUSSIES!!!

Friday 4/10/98

Well a lot has happened. A whole month – two have flown by. I hate lacrosse – I could have seen that coming (we had to go to St. Petersburg, FL to practice over spring break). Last night was a wonderful and horrifying experience at the same time. I was high – so high that I couldn't function – it was an awesome experience, I felt orgasmic almost – was so good. I couldn't even talk – I could mutter constants, but that was about it.

The horrible experience was that I really believe these two guys were going to rape me – they thought I was passed out – yeah right, not that stupid –(they started taking off my pants and then I kicked the one in face and said that I was awake and had heard what they said the whole time) that is BAD, really bad, Angie found out and told the Dean of Student Affairs and there will definitely be trouble for them. My only concern is Fred – what to do about Fred, he left me in the room w/ them when he knew what they were going to try and do – he left me there! Vince came down and was my hero – he is great!

Wednesday 5/20/98

Sophomore year is over – Seniors have graduated. Much has happened of corse.

1) Lacrosse – ECAC champs – big deal!
2) High – new hobby? not really
3) Boys – still a problem.
4) Combo of 2+3 NOT good

The night before the seniors graduated – an experience – old friend Jake! Zach – hmm, that's odd, someones little brother. STOS "I thought we hated each other?" (I was lying down on a bunk bed somewhere in APEs with my eyes shut and he came up and was starring at me thinking I was asleep and then he leaned over and started kissing me when he thought I was asleep. I just kept pretending I was asleep and he stopped). That weekend before graduation was full of surprises, enough to last the whole summer. Laura and I were high together – It was neat – highness is scary.

Summer – I hate jobs, I have a job at the Ice House with Joanna – it sucks, but this guy is really flirty w/ me – Ron, 28, definite looser – yet I still find him very physically attractive and he seems to think I am God's gift to the world – which is always nice. I hate that the most attractive quality I can find in guys is that they find me attractive – sounds like a desperate person to me – definitely need to change that.

Tuesday 6/23/98

Months go by so fast! Summer has begun. Funny thing – Ron disappeared – not a great loss. Saw Brendon at fun days – we went out, not really out – to his apartment in Reading. He just wanted to see if he could have sex with me – denied – obviously, so that was the end of that. I visited Laura a couple of weeks ago. I have no concept of time these days. We had fun – went to some guy's party and were being ourselves. She got into some political discussion about women's rights, while my attentions were more focused on the naked people on T.V. I love visiting Laura, her family life is so healthy, and she has guy friends, something I seem to lack! All I do these days are work and sleep – my dreams are the only eventful place. Last night I dreamt that college had started and I was in my room – a single – in some dorm. I was at college but not Brynell – it was different. Then Scott came in – he said I was in the wrong room. Then I went to the room next to his – which was mine and it was a storage type room – all the washing machines and dryers were in there, I was so upset. Then all of a sudden the scene flashed and I was in a new room that was nicer, but still supposed to be a storage room but it was bigger and there were lots of pictures all over the wall. I remember seeing pink a lot and pigs. My bed from home was brought in, and Scott was helping. I couldn't figure out where to put the bed. I remember being so excited about Scott living next door. Then he and I were outside running around and even though my room looked like an attic room the ground was right outside. Scott was saying how he was going to creep up near my window at night and scare me and we were laughing. Then all the sudden I was at a stadium – some game was going on and Deanna from work walked by and she told me that they were selling coke at Wallmart. I asked her what they were selling it in and she wouldn't tell me. Then I looked down and she had a box full of containers of glitter – so then I said "The coke is in the glitter." Then I was back in my room again – there were other people there, but I don't know who they were. We were all sitting around watching some movie. I had this kind of high tech system – with two T.V.s – one was really narrow horizontally and I remember there was a really green couch. Then the movie went fuzzy. And I remember being really scared that the werewolf was going to come get me? Strange I thought. Aaah, I am 20 – not a teenager, not a kid – but not old enough yet.

Thursday 6/25/98

On Tuesday Kristen and I were hanging around – bored, had off, decided to get a little tipsy. I ended up calling a lot of people – no one was home, though Jason's mom answered – I didn't leave a message. Well, to my surprise I was awoken the next morning at 9:00am to a phone call – it was Jason! Could you believe, they have caller ID! We ended up talking for about 2 hrs it was nice. I am not sure what will come out of this new occurrence – though very needed in this not so extraordinary life.

Tuesday 7/14/98

Boring – everything is absolutely boring, not to mention wrong. Scott is transferring – great, I am sad. School is giving me a freshman roomate – whoopee and I have 2 extra teeth above each of my upper wisdom teeth (one above each) – 1,000 dollars to remove!

There is nothing to look forward to at school. I had a dream about Scott the other night. We were in my old room at the old house. He gave me the head to his hockey stick and a softball, that he called a baseball, and a glove. We were hugging, and then he kissed me – that's the first time he's ever kissed me – in my dreams!

Joanna and I went on our 4 day vacation last week – not really a vacation. We went to Wildwood 1st – rode the rides at night and ended up sleeping in the car. We went to the water park the next day and beach again and then to Stone Habor to stay with Lynn + Stacia – my loving sorority sisters. We slept on the floor there with one of the residents, Jen's, younger brothers!
The last night there we went to visit Vince and Mike from APEs in Ocean City. They have their own place with a couple of friends. I had my back scratched by this awkwardly funny guy, Tony. They all had the wrong impression, as usual!

Ignorance is bliss
Thought provokes concern.
I will always want more.
I am absolutely psychotic, the 1st part of this diary is written in pencil – why – because I didn't want to "mess up" – in my own personal diary. I have problems.
I really despise my mother –
I hate how when you make a doctors apt for say 2:30pm you most definitely will not get to see the doctor until after 3:00 – why do they do that – If my apt says 2:30 I want to see the doctor at 2:30, that's why your just a little bit early. Why can't they get it right?

Sunday 8/9/98
Josh – weirdo. A summer fling I suppose. I never liked him in the 1st place and it took me 2 weeks to finally realize this. I just decided not to call him anymore. Though he did have one really good quality – Yes he definitely did. So last night I went

over to Laura's party – was fun and all her friends were there – nothing super but nice. We were drunk and they got me to go in the hot tub with them – in my britches. Then he showed up – Mr. Dream Guy from Princeton – wow! He got in the hot tube w/ me. We chatted about school and sports – he was very friendly + nice and before I knew it, it was just us two in the tub and well, we had some fun. I really liked him – he was so friendly and polite, not to mention gorgeous. Now that I have had a taste of the grander – I want that! That is the type that I will marry – yuppers – NO MORE LOOSERS FOR ME!!

Monday 9/14/98

     School has begun – had classes for about 2 weeks now. They are alright. I've kissed 4 boys already – darnit, I just get a little bit selfish when I come back to college – like a kid in a candy store, all these cutie boys to choose from. Of course 3 of them are in APEs, urgh. I can't seem to get away from those football guys. The 4th is from Lehigh. That was a very interesting night. Joanna and I both hooked up about 3 ft from one another. I think it is funny. Boys are dumb.

     Lynn lives in the house. I like her very much – enough to bring her home to dinner with Grandma – we had fun. My cousin was there. I'm glad Lynn is in the house. I have a single and it is very nicely set up. The "BOOTY PAD" I guess.

     The other night Tom and I sat up in my room for at least an hour and talked about life and college (he thought we were each other's first hookup at college back when he was a 304 football guy and Killer wanted something dramatic to watch). He must have been very impressed about our conversation because he proclaims to everyone his admiration for me – how he "loves" me and that I am a "down to earth" girl. This makes me feel good inside. I can't remember when a guy has spoken so highly of me – maybe no one has before.

I care about Vince, though I don't know how to handle this?

Today I spoke with Marvin from work. He might visit me this weekend – I would like that very much. He is a nice guy.

This past weekend a guy, by the name of Sam, and I had good conversation. He said he would take me to the Baltimore Harbor for the whole day, then to a nice restaurant. I didn't find him that attractive though I found what he said to me extremely attractive. He is 24, has a secure job, and would like a nice girl to take out. What he proposed to me was an actual date, with dinner and the works. I don't think I have ever really been on a "real" date! I decided to give him my phone # anyway – though I feel guilty because even though he is a wonderful guy, who thought the world of me I will never go out with him because of his appearance – I am a horrible person for that.

Scott was up this weekend. I love him, I love being around him, I love him touching me, laughing at what I say, looking into my eyes, I feel utterly secure when I am with him and nobody is around. I would be with him for the rest of my life even if he would never even kiss me, as long as he could look into my eyes and put his arms around me. I want so badly to hold his face in my hands and tell him that I care for him more than any other man I've known. I don't know what love is or if I love him, I only know that when I am around him I get that feeling inside that is so different than anything I have ever felt. I can never tell him any of this for it would scare him and make him uncomfortable and I could possibly loose him. He is my father, brother, and love combined into one. To know that I will never be his lover; that he will never look at me that way brings tears to my heart that fill my eyes. I've tried and I can't get over him, I don't think I will ever be able to forget him for the rest of my life.

Thursday 12/10/98

The months fly by so fast ironically the last time I wrote was when Scott was up – he is up again though I have not seen him. I've kissed a few boys – only 3 or 4 – not many – I've only been in APE's house once – and I spent that time in the bathroom, not feeling too well. Indoor track has begun – I like it – the people are very nice – almost all are freshman. John runs – sophomore – was Pete's roomate – nice guy – we spent one hour talking together at dinner – I didn't even notice, but everyone else left the table. I think I have feelings toward him – yeah I do – I'm afraid I don't want to start something because I see him every day at practice – he is so nice and we get along so well.

I am so busy these days – classes, practice, work – I have no life during the weeks – finals are next week – everything goes by so fast.

I haven't seen much of Laura lately – Lynn has become one of my very good friends – I like her! I feel good about myself lately – I feel that I have done well – probably because I am exercising everyday – that always makes me feel as though I have accomplished something. I've been getting along with boys well – haven't tried to kill any lately – ha ha. The formal is on Sat. I am taking Noah from Demas – he is very kind – I hope that he gets along well with everyone – I am not into entertaining people. I'm not sad- not that happy – just doing alright. I need to STOP talking to Neil – lost cause – I really don't know why I do? I talked to Damon at our rush on sat – that was weird, yet healthy. I just want to be friends with everyone. I have this horrible dumb problem – physical – don't need to talk about that anymore – it is kind of humorous Grandma laughed at me when I told her that I thought only old people got these!

Friday 4/2/99

Time has flown by – I have braces – decided to invest in my teeth – got them on in Feb (Feb 1st). I haven't kissed any boy's for the New Year – the last one was Jeff – Dragon University on New Year's Eve – things about that later. Tonight I stole a chicken. Leigh and I saved a chicken from a horrid life. POD had a chicken (they got at an auction) that they were torturing – giving beer and not feeding. Leigh and I stole the chicken from their common room and drove it to the safety of a nearby farm. They probably don't even know yet that it is gone!

Sunday 6/6/99

Junior year is over now. It was a good year. I have put myself in sexual detox! I am sick of society demeaning my sexuality as it does to all women. Therefore, I am in total control of my sexuality, literally and figuratively! I have not even kissed a boy in over 6 months now. Also – no sex for over two years, however, there should of never been any sex to begin with, I guess we learn from our mistakes. A naïve 18 year old girl is very different from a three year college educated 21 year old woman. My desire is mine; it does not belong to any man. I love myself and I rejoice in my own experiences.

This past weekend was great. Thursday we went to Dragon University. Jeff and Matt attempted to be suitors – if they could be called that, however, neither was successful – they never even had a chance. Friday was great – I learned a lot about my friends/sisters – We played "never have I ever" which inevitably becomes an extremely sexually revealing game for participants. We all promised not to lie – when the taboo question of masturbation arose – we all, except one, drank. I was amazed and relieved. I had never really believed that other people, rather other girls did (I didn't even discover this ability until the beginning of my sophomore year because of Judd, oh Judd, no wonder I was so out of control my freshman year). I think is it wonderful, however, we all admit that we would never forfeit this information to any boyfriends or males! We have all played the game before with guys and lied through our teeth on this information – why do we do this? Because we have to, because our culture says that we need to be non-sexual – we cannot lust and desire – we have to be in control to negotiate male overtures. Society puts women in the role of controlling sex - if we then also desire sex, as much or maybe more so than men, then society will be sexual chaos. If it was alright for men and women to be promiscuous then sex would be rampant – or so it seems. Not like it isn't now. I like the idea of masturbation (the power!!) because it allows women to explore sexuality without men. One more way in which we don't need men anymore – ha

 I will now be a senior – what a horrid thought – graduation. I have no idea what I want to do – but I don't want to be average in any sense of the word. One topic that is of great interest to me as I learn more and more about is sexuality – so taboo to society. I think the "shock value" makes me like it more and more. The more I learn the more I want to explore, however the less I actually do.

Wednesday 8/4/99

 Yes, I returned to the shore, to North Wildwood – land of firsts for me. Leigh and I spent a week at the shore – full of alcohol and dancing. We went out every night to whatever club Joe had recommended. It was great! I was determined to keep w/ with my sexual fasting, even when temptation occurred Sunday night – Moore's – I met a wonderful guy – Steven. We danced all night, it seemed like we spent every moment together. He noticed me when Leigh and I had decided to request our favorite song by Stardust – "music sounds better w/ you." Apparently the crowd there at that time was not amused by our song, so we ended up dancing by ourselves –in front of the whole bar. He started dancing w/ us and then me. He was a good dancer and I enjoyed dancing w/ him. Towards the end of the night the song (an "oldie") about run around Sue came on. I had always wanted to dance to that song the way Julia Roberts and her new costar had in

"Sleeping w/ the Enemy." We danced to it. He spun me around and dipped me. I loved every minute of it. As I was leaving and we were slow dancing He started to kiss me, I let it happen for about 2 seconds but then pulled away. I wanted to remain sexually fasting. Maybe he will call and maybe he won't, but I had my moment, I was Julia Roberts dancing in the movie.

Each night was full of surprises. There were new people around every corner. This wasn't the time to be shy.

One night Leigh and I had drunk a bit too much. When we were leaving the bar there had been a fight and we weren't paying attention to where we were walking. All the sudden we realized that we were lost, we had started going towards the bridge. It didn't matter to us though we began to flail about defacing property in the early morning. I or should I even say we ripped down an American flag off of someone's flagpole – how rebellious – I shoved the flag into the front of my pants mistakenly thinking that it would not be obvious to anyone what we had done, though the bulge was very apparent and suspicious looking. We finally made it home that night after breaking and entering into a lifeguard's house that Leigh had, should we say, previously met.

My sexual fasting, which began Jan 1, 1998 was about to change. On Thursday night we were at a club – the theme for the night was "what the buck," any drink for a dollar. Well as one can imagine we took advantage of this cheap theme. I met a lot of guys, they were all friendly, to say the least, but one was different. He was tall, with white blond curly hair in a fro. He had freckles. He was wearing a white T-shirt, probably with some logo of which I forget, and board shorts. I asked him his name and he said "Hook." Well that did it for me. This guy was different, and I like different. We talked and I asked him where he went to school – he replied "I went to the school of hard knocks baby." He didn't say it suavely – just nonchalantly as he gazed around the club, perhaps avoiding my eyes for fear of my expression to his comment. I initiated things further. I asked him if he had ever swum in the ocean at night. He replied "of course," this was expected since he was a local. I said that I had never been and he stated "lets go." As we walked out to the ocean I told him about my new year's resolution, about my rule of not kissing of not "hooking up." I was still determined to keep my new 6 month old rule in effect. He undressed first and ran into the ocean, his bottom ghostly white, shinned out through the darkness. I then undressed quickly and ran in while trying to over those parts that are not to be seen with my arms. We were both in the water, it was cold but exhilarating

I swam about joking how I resembled the beginning of "Jaws" and that I would be very upset if a shark was to come along at that time. He stood in the waves watching me. The moon was full that night. It glistened off the water with a trail that lead strait into the horizon. Everything was dark except for the brightness of the moon. We were close to each other. He grew nearer to me and I thought that I should stay away but I didn't. He stood right in front of me, we were waist deep in the pitch black water. He looked at me and said "I don't like your rule." His hands slid up onto my face, cupping my head. I knew what was about to happened, but I didn't stop him. He drew me to him and we kissed and embraced each other. I can just imagine how beautiful we looked, our naked bodies embraced with the lights of the full moon glistening off our skin and dancing in the waves. I know it was a gorgeous sight. After the kiss I paused and reflected on the greatness of the moment, how it was perfect, how for that instant I had achieved perfection. It was beautiful.

We stayed in for a little while longer. I went out first and got dressed quickly. As we walked back towards the club and through town I wondered if it was obvious what we had done by our wet clothes and my dripping hair. It didn't matter to me, I almost wanted people to know that we had been devious, how we defied authority and societal norms. I looked for Leigh but I could not find her. We began walking toward my house. I wondered if he would walk with me the whole way. I thought I should take advantage of this situation. I had already defied my sexual fasting by kissing him, why not experience more. I had never made out in the grass before. This is what I decided we should do. He didn't argue. We found a spot on the corner of a street. There was landscaping and center pieces of shrubbery. This was perfect. We crept behind the brush. He laid his shirt on the grass which he had taken off earlier while we were walking through town. We both lied down. The grass thrilled me – the idea that anyone who glanced over in the right direction could see us being mischievous. We rolled around for an hour or so. My shorts came off but nothing risky happened. He, of course, urged for more but I denied. I was content with rolling around in the grass. I walked over to a near bush to relieve my bladder which had built up from the alcohol consumption at the bar. When I walked back over he had fallen asleep. He was lying on his back with his arms across his chest and his hands under his armpits. He looked so peaceful. I couldn't wake him. I put my shorts on and began home. I wonder when he awoke and what he thought. I would love to have seen what happened. Howard, that was his name. I know his last name was French and it was something like that.

Once we began rolling around together I realized that I was sexually ravenous. I loved his touch, his feel. I had forgotten what this feels like to be so close together. I told him that I was ravenous – I don't think he understood. That's okay I needed to feel something that I hadn't for a long time. The following night, Friday night, Leigh and I had gone out again. This was our last night out. We drank and we danced. I danced knowing that I am a good dancer, knowing that eyes were all over me when there was no one else on the floor but Leigh and I. Later I was told that that was when he was watching me, when he was starring.

Leigh and I were making our rounds. Chatting and making friends with new people. I noticed she had started talking w/ two guys that were standing near the bar we were at. She introduced me to them and told me that the one was a lifeguard. He was 6'4" and tan. He had white blond hair, which appeared to be dyed and bright white teeth. He almost looked like a doll. There were no flaws in his features. When Leigh told me that he was a lifeguard I laughed and stated how I hated all the lifeguards. Even though I appeared to be kidding, there was more truth to that statement then he could have ever acknowledged. He looked upset by my statement so I apologized and replied that it was stereotypical of me to say that to him. I explained that I had good reason without any further details. We talked. He didn't attend school. He was 22 and I wondered why he wasn't in school. He looked as though he came from money with his perfect features, button down pale blue shirt and khaki shorts. We went out to the dance floor and danced. He had said that he was a good dancer but he actually wasn't very good at all. We walked around chatting and talking with Leigh. She had met a few guys that she had known in high school. We were all talking and I heard one of the other guys ask Jeff- the lifeguard "is that your girl" pointing toward me. He replied with a nod stating "yeah." I was his girl. What did this mean? We obviously weren't dating. We had just met and now I was his girl. This peaked my curiosity. I told him that I wanted to go swimming in the ocean. We left.

We walked out to the ocean. It looked different. It didn't have the glow it did the night before. It didn't feel beautiful to me as it had the night before. He undressed and walked in. He was tall and lanky, much thinner than he appeared to be in his clothing. I watched him. I could not follow, it didn't feel right. For an instance I thought to run, run away, and leave him in the water. To take all of his clothes so that he would be naked and trapped. This would be a revenge on all lifeguards – he would be my revenge. But I didn't do it. I stayed and watched him as he walked out of the ocean asking me what I was doing and why I hadn't gone in. I turned as he put his clothes on. He looked confused. He was very insecure. I was surprised by this. He was extremely attractive yet he had no attitude of such. He was not as mentally strong as me. I had all the power, I felt bad for him. We embraced. I put my arms around his body and he put his around my back and shoulders – we fit perfectly – it was worth it. No sex – just feeling each other

Friday 10/15/99

Senior year has begun. The first weekend was rough – too much vodka – but I have learned now. No more attending Brynell parties – to the bar for me. I like being the youngest there – all new people – it is very exciting. I've met a few people – some have called. Yesterday in fact I had a message from Paul – very, no, extremely attractive man. Built very well w/ blond hair, he waited about 3 weeks to call, but I would like to see what happens.

Judd, yes he is back yet again. Though, I have a weird feeling about him – almost like he has drastically changed. I've talked to him about three times on the phone in the past three weeks. The last conversation was genuine. He was sincere in what he said and we actually had a long "normal" conversation. He told me about his life and what he wants to do and I did the same. The girls in the house don't think very highly of him. I didn't either until the last talk we had. There is just something about him that tells me I need to keep him around??? – You know I love those blondes.

Judd is going to be up this weekend for homecoming. I am glad – I want to see him, actually I really want to see him because I have been thinking about this all week. We were very blatant on the phone about seeing each other alone ….. ha ha ha I hope everything goes well – please don't let him screw anything up!!

Leigh is awesome – I love her to death. I love all the girls in the house. I am so glad that they are my friends – even though they pick on me sometimes – or often for that matter, I don't know what my life would be like w/ out them. Each one adds something to me – makes me a better person – and makes me want to strive for more. I really will miss these simple nights that we spend together after we graduate. I feel really bad and guilty because I know I am hard to live with and I know I am stubborn w/ a hatred complex for myself – but none of them ever give up on me - they don't quit so neither can I!

I look to Leigh to be loved, to Lynn for leadership, to Laura for cuddles and dancing, to Stacia for boldness, to Elizabeth for sternness, to Brooke for intellectualness, to Leslie for laughter, and to Annie for innocence. I am scared to lose so much for fast.

I look at my past and it wasn't as nice as it could have been, yet it wasn't that bad. I didn't realize that until I was older, that things are not given. Assumptions can be challenged – nothing is definite, and not all is what it seems. Textbooks are only perceptions of ideas and actions. Information is biased and ideals change over time. What is knowledge today is forgotten tomorrow.

What I know is that I need love in my life of some form at all times, I need to feel love, to see love, and experience love. Most of all, I must learn to love myself at all times because I need that love first and forth right.

I search to find love among the blank faces of men, yet, I already know that I must love myself first before they even have a chance. I have to love my teeth (braces and all) my face, my skin, my curly hair, my body, my lanky long legs and my big feet. My face is the part of my body that saddens me the most. I feel that my face has failed me. That I have to fix it – that it is wrong, this isn't the way I was supposed to look. However, the experiences that I have gone through – I know have formed my life. When you feel unattractive you must build yourself around other characteristics. I chose achievement – I love to achieve. I don't believe that I am fully unattractive now – yet I am not by any means finished.

I remember what people have said to me like it was yesterday. The boys on the baseball field in 9th grade whispered just loud enough when I was walking by so that I could hear. John H. in 5th grade laughed hysterically at me when I suggested that he liked me. In 11th grade Justin turned directly to my face and told me that I was disgusting. Cole screamed at me that I would never be his girlfriend – that he didn't want to date me at all. These few examples – the ones that I remember most vividly – have created me. I am a bitter person – I have a lot of rage – especially for men, I more than anything, would love to rip those people apart. But what bothers me more is that I remember this – I let them get to me – like they won. And I can't let it go – I will never forget hearing this guy Barten say that he would only call me if he needed an organ because he was dying. I never deserved for people to be so cruel to me. I think about this constantly, that I am a failure. I play it off to my "family" that I don't care – but I do – I do a lot. I feel like there's something wrong with me – that I am defective and I blame this mostly on the way I look – my skin – my teeth. Normal people have good skin and nice teeth – and that is what I want – I don't want to be less than average or mediocre. I hate feeling that way. When people look at me I want to exude confidence – but I don't.

Tuesday 2/29/00

So much is changing. It's amazing how one day someone can be such a necessary part of your life and the next day they are gone. I no longer speak to Joanna, Leigh and I aren't close – our personalities clash, I don't trust Leslie at all – she betrayed my trust *(and not to mention the senior sorority cruise over winter break to New Orleans, Cozumel, and the Caymen Islands was a little dramatic. When we went to New Orleans I was with my little cruise ship guy that I met who was on the cruise with his entire family for the holidays. Well we went to Pat Obrien's for lunch and his father got us ridiculously drunk buying us these hurricane drinks and then he sets us free into the streets of New Orleans. We barely made it back to the ship. Literally we were running for the ship and Wade was screaming at me to run faster, that we were going to miss it! After we got on completely winded and ready to*

~ 80 ~

collapse they pulled up the gate and I was like holly fuck I'm the last person on the ship! I have no idea what we he and I did all day?).

I have learned that to create your own reality of your life you must dictate what is known to the outside and what is known to you. I choose to recall those events that I want, if others know differently – they contradict that reality I have created. I have realized that my childhood caused me great emotional harm, however because I have somewhat been able to overcome this, I have no sympathy for other people. If I did it, why can't they. I don't do anything that I am not satisfied with. I am not engaging or w/ concern for others because I literally and sincerely do not care and I won't do something lacking sincerity. I don't play the game very well. The most I can do is say "how are you" when passing by an acquaintance.

I have learned that everyone perceives their world differently. When I look into the mirror I am myself as I see myself. Another's perception of me and my physical characteristics can be totally different than my own. What people "see" isn't just as it is, it is their minds perception of images, which can in turn change from person to person.

Things that I remember
- driving golf carts + Zima
- night with Vince (the king made me feel so good)
- love ritual
- date
- graveyard + Tom + Dave
- Leslie and Brooke
- Elizabeth
- late night discussions w/ Brooke and Laura
- knowing that I am better than what I do
- That which does not kill me makes me stronger

Sex – so consuming – so virile – physical – that's all I know – that's all I can express. For 2000 it has become intense – primal – unrepressed + ravenous, yet still intolerable. My behavior – I feel that it's unacceptable, disgusting and grotesque. I am frustrated and impatient, waiting for love, for someone to love me – that leaves me with no control. I can be physical – no love, no emotion because I am ignorant to it. I have never experienced it, therefore to me it is ideal, it's perfect, therefore I disgust myself because I give away that perfection. I also fear – no love, never to be loved, age, all will fade. I want to relish in my physicality now, in my youth, when I am passionate.

Thursday 5/18/00

Back to the beginning of March, yes, the love ritual I think provocatively worked. Not to attract love, yet sex, and a lot of it. The past 2 months have been a ridiculous blur of men, some that I would like to remember and some that I wouldn't. The first was Dragon University, Logan, Trent – 2nd – yes, I was the predator... I have had a thing for him, and I just let go. Then Dicky in Olin hall – an academic building – how sur-real (this classroom is actually in the beginning of "How to Get Away with Murder"- we were right there on a table up where the professor presents in front!). The trick is that night, Tim soon followed. I just wanted to see if I could have two in one night. Then just a few days later it was Nate, sweet, lovely, naïve Nate. Things went a bit far, but I have yet to count that as the first time, but, apparently he does. A mere 2 days later it was Joshua L. at Dragon. I was hesitant, but not sure why. I have mixed feelings to this occurrence. I was not the predator, the attacker, the seducer who gets what she wants; however, I must still count it. Within one week I experienced four different men; how morally awful, yet, deliciously interesting. Then I was off to Boston with some of the sorority girls for some culture. No men there, just experiences of intellectual gratification. We saw a play starring Matthew Broderick (Ferris

Bueller) that was humorous. Also we went to Pravda, which later we found to realize was an "exclusive" vodka bar in the Boston area. We unknowingly entered confident and cheerful, not realizing we were lucky to be allowed in. It even got more interesting when Brooke and I went to find the restroom and stumbled into a whole new back room of the bar that was hidden around a corner and hallway. It was a scene from a movie when we found the corner. Our eyes widened, mouths dropped and all we could do is look at each other in awe. It was like we found treasure. The vampire bar! We went to another bar because Brooke wanted to go – Lava – a gay bar. Brooke managed to talk down the cover charge of 10$ to zero with some baseball antics. The bar was hot and crowded, nothing really enticed me there – I liked Pravda much better.

  After returning, I just stuck with Nate. Everything was my effort. You know that we never end in something positive. He has good intentions, I believe, but he's so young, in all respects. He was more interested in being my friend then my lover. Nate would say that I attacked him – I like saying that I attack, however, the prey should never refer to it as that, such a negative term. He was resistant and uninviting accept for two times. The night that we went to Susan's - the bonfire - he pulled me onto his lap. The other night was the formal - which I don't recall much from later. The last few days were weird. I don't think he is mature enough to realize all I could offer him. And I neglected to tell myself how limited he is because of his niceness and pretty face framed upon a 6'2" prime body. He left - not finding me or leaving any information. I have no qualms that he will think about me. He has the reminders of pictures and Jack posters as reminders. He will realize one day. However, there is more wrong about him than right. I know he was looking for me because of the housemate across the hall. That is enough for me to be appeased with this departure. I am not upset because I fully believe that he just does not realize or comprehend there is a large possibility he may never see me again.

Nate left me on my birthday. In my confusion I attacked, what was there, any attractive male. Due to the numerous vodka filled drinks I don't recall all the activity that night. Yet from key pictures in my mind I know what happened and I am bitter and angry. That should not happen to me. Especially on the celebration of the day I was born.

April was calmer than March. I was in pursuit of Nate. He was my new obsession. We were only together a few times. The last was the formal. I have positive thoughts about him. I love that he would say "Aww Mary." The night before graduation takes the cake - it was a humdinger. Dicky found me. We slipped off to his room. We had always joked about the pole vault mats due to our track background together. Well that was going to be my going away present. After some gracious activity in his room we then prowled over towards the field, however, due to the over powering lights making it easy to get caught, we decided to take a new route. The baseball field, yes, center field, right behind the home-run barrier. It was incredible, ripping and grasping contorted bodies, and unbelievable synchrony. A final, everlasting memory of college, Dicky - who offered Olin and center field. What a guy. I was satisfied with that. I slid back into the party at Zack's. Laura turned to me and asked where I was. I nonchalantly say, "oh, I've been mingling." Which she, more easily than I thought, accepted. With bruised knee's I begin talking and chatting, as if nothing happened. I ran into a guy who attended high school with me, Mark. I was always friendly w/ him because of the similar background. Little did I know. Zack's ran out of beer. We all returned to the house for the advent of the traditional Tau Sig/O'Chi sorority softball game. We headed down, and the game manifested itself very differently this year. It became the girls versus the baseball team. We were in our bras and shorts, they were in their boxers. It was fun, and interesting. After the game I ventured over to 702, which I know is not beneficial for me yet, I relish in the torture. I like to complicate things, ruffle some feathers and see the reaction. People's behavior is strangely alluring. I talked with Vince and Bird Boy. Someone made a comment, as usual, because of their ignorance. However, it is their ignorance and not mine. Mark was there. I don't remember where he came from or when he came over to me, but we started chatting. I suspected intentions, but I played along because of my fascination w/ behavior and what would happen next. I watched people disappear one by one as we remained on the couch outside together. Most left when APEs went on their naked golfing spree. We were left. He began, it was started when he said he was going to sleep in his car. I then offered that there was plenty of room in 702, the frat house, but he denied. I knew where this was leading. I offered my roommates bed and he accepted. We went over and I began preparing the bed. He stopped me and said he wouldn't feel comfortable. Then he was in my bed. I jokingly said not to get fresh. I knew his ploy. I rolled over not facing him. Maybe I could fall asleep. Nope, his hands began to roam, I made no movement pretending that I was asleep (same thing I had done during freshman pledging when they gave us to the fraternity and the senior pledge master made me sleep next to him). I rolled over to show that my eyes were closed so that he would think I was asleep. Nope, didn't work. I could feel his hot breath on my face, so close, I was a mouse, seconds from the cats attack, no escape possible. He rubbed his nose against mine. I know. We kissed! Gentle and slow. He is very loving. No clothes removed, nothing adventurous just gentle holding, kissing, and a bit of roaming hands. It was what I had desperately wanted from Nate that he never offered. I didn't get any sleep. We stayed embraced, as stroked my back, arm, head. He was never motionless, always wanting to please. I wonder if I was planned for him. If I was something that he had to have before I left. I don't know if he is that way with everyone, but, I felt wonderful. He acted towards me as if he was in love with me. He left and I began preparing for graduation.

Graduation was as unstimulating as I had thought; too many references to God and family. I appreciate my education. I realize how people are taught what they should believe instead of finding it for themselves. I chose to find my belief through strenuous realizations. I do not believe in God, yet, Nature as an energy and continuous force. I control my life and its occurrences. Religion is used by society to constrain people, give them preformed values and ideas that they can easily slide into; a pre-fit mold. I won't accept that. Society, marriage, especially sex, must all be reconsidered. I do what I believe. Sex is beautiful, and should be practiced as an enlightening experience (Frederick Engles would agree). Constraints are made by the fearful, not I. Relish in the pleasures of the body. I love my body and all its capability. It is beautiful, yet, the most beautiful part is the mind, it still remains to be the greatest instrument, and also the greatest sexual instrument. It's hard to say what many would say of my actions. A slut, possibly, but they have not considered all that I have. I will age. My body could wrinkle and sag. Yet, I will relish in how I was and those who shared in joy and pleasure offered. My body is not everything, yet, it is my greatest instrument. With this last semester of college, I felt it was time to engage myself, my form, to its fullest extent. Those who see it negatively may not comprehend this type of transcendence to move beyond societal constraints or perhaps they are simply jealous of my vivaciousness.

Second Diary

July 13, 2000

I've graduated, yes college is over. I've done it – a degree, an apartment, a job, a new car. I'm not a failure and that's how I would put it. I don't consider myself successful. I always need to do more, there can always be improvement, always.

It appears that I live the fantasy life of the 20s, or should I say 20 year olds. Independent, young, so-called beautiful, yet, I am still angry, still bitter. I only remember the hurt. The things I had to go through that no one else in the entire world can ever comprehend. Yes, I am happy. Probably the happiest I have ever been, away from my past, away from people that remind me of what used to be. My feelings are so complex. I don't think I can understand or verbalize them. I have a love/hate relationship with my past. I hate that I am angry for my mentally insufficient, selfish mother, abandoning father, emotionally unfulfilling grandparents and cruel, unhearted "men."

July 19, 2000

Well, I've done it again, a meaningless fuck, in the back of my grandmother's station wagon - some random dude that I apparently attacked. I am a predator, a sexual predator wanting to satisfy and insatiable sexual appetite. In doing so I push the "right" guys away and attract the "wrong" ones. I was wasted, which I don't use as an excuse, however, I am amazed at how I can act, it's almost as if I have multiple personalities. I set these sexual goals for myself, yet, I break them. I just don't know what to think?

Now, I must speak of Ryan, tender, sweet, caring Ryan. He is nothing like me, though no one is ever like me. Why do I always push so much to be physical. I've realized that I do this over and over. I've even done this with Ryan, however, he knew what I was doing and stopped me. What if I just have no emotional attachment to sexual activity? I think I have only had sex once or twice sober, and that was with the first one. Am I obsessed? Ryan is a reality check it seems. He is not transcended nor is he philosophical. He has the contemporary belief that to have sex each partner should care about the other. I find that appealing, while at the same time I am still drawn to the concept of free sexuality, perhaps known as the term "whore" or "slut" for women!

I feel horrible that this random action occurred one week after I had met Ryan. I didn't intend to do anything. Why do things happen the most when you don't even plan? I feel as though I ruin everything or perhaps sabotage myself?

Ryan came over last night, cooked me dinner, caressed my head and arms later and brought me to an unrealistic climax with his gently touch. I fear that he is not raw, not virile. I want someone to want me so badly that they cannot by any means resist. Ryan does not display this kind of rawness. In consideration of his age, he is older, almost four years, and that may lead to more of an impulse control, but I still want the rawness!

August 13, 2000

All is well! I have won. UC by the Sea – all my former APEs were in attendance. Judd, the mere gesture that he came over to me, that when we both motioned for each other to come over, he came to me. Both times – I have won. The game is now over with this mere gesture. He even came to my window and threw pebbles to wake me from my slumber upon the eve of our salvation.

Ryan is well. He is attentive, caring, gentle and generous, qualities that are not my strongest. We are opposites in so many different arenas. I like when he holds me, I feel so wanted and loved, and this coming from a man is so extraordinary for me. I am starting to become attached and this frightens me.

I feel like I have everything, but there is still something missing. It's like when you travel and you just have a feeling that something was left behind. I don't know what it is but I am worried that I won't be able to get rid of this feeling and it will ruin everything.

October 7, 2000

Today is homecoming at Brynell College, and ironically, Ryan's birthday. Although not fully realizing it at the time, I broke up with Ryan last night. I had known for a while that he wasn't what I was looking for. I am glad that I found him, I was able to gain a great deal from the three months that we were together. Ryan is very loving and caring, however, I do not find him stimulating or intriguing, rather he is secure and stable. He's shown me that men can be caring and emotionally sensitive beings, even more so than I had ever imagined. He was weak and I was strong. I never displayed strong emotion in the sense that I was not able to control my situation. People become cumbersome when they fail to entice me anymore. I am presently in a vertigo. I know what I want to do with my future. I want to teach, women's studies/gender issues. To inform the world of the wrongs of society and implications for women (x and y). I will write a book "Reclaiming Society: The Inherent Female" – the genetically inferior female, also known as the male. I can know this, yet, not know what my future holds for next week. As this brings me to what occurred last night.

After I had stated that I was leaving to Ryan I went to the young alumni gathering at the local bar. All expected people were in attendance, especially my APEs. Now, this is usual for them to be at an alumni function in such large numbers since most of them live in the past trying to relive their drawn out prime of college. What is unusual is Jake having a three hour in depth, philosophical, analytical conversation. I am perplexed, thrown into my vertigo of awareness and perception. People will and can amaze me.

I fear Jake. I fear him in that the way that I felt in 7th grade after Dave. Dave was my "boyfriend" in 7th grade for a week or so. He was my boyfriend, or should I say that we were "going out" and people, peers, made fun of him for going out with me. My peers were so effective with this that Dave broke up with me and then that day wrote me a note that said – I want to go out with you but don't tell anyone. I will never forget this. Even though this can be expected from a 7th grader, I feel that this situation relives itself over and over in my life. Because I choose not to conform to societal norms I am labeled as different. An aggressive, dominating, intelligent woman can be very intimidating to college men especially. I feel that in college I never had a boyfriend because of how I was labeled. Now that I have graduated does that change? Jake said last night after our conversation that he loved me, not in a necessarily romantic sense, yet, in an intellectual, "I like that you think like me" sense. Today, however, in the midst of everyone's socializing he wasn't as nearly as responsive to me as the previous night. Does this mean that someone who is so compatible with me will never be able to overcome the prejudice of others towards me? I won't be anyone's secret girlfriend and I know, I really know that he meant everything he said to me last night. He likes my mind, the way I think, and that is not something a person can falsify or pretend to do. Why bother, what is the gratification? His statements about me where true because I enlightened him to my beliefs on society of which he understood and agreed.

I am supposed to call him and I am so scared. I fear I will be hurt. With him I am going to have a wall so high and so thick that he will and must strain himself in every way to see what I have hidden from him. I will show no emotion of sadness, no weakness, and no loving either.

December 24, 2000

So many things can change in such a short amount of time. In the middle and end of October I withdrew myself into a depression. Jake withered away as I had suspected and I grew very sad and disappointed at myself for what I had done to Ryan. On Halloween, a very powerful Wiccan night, I could not fake it any longer and I called Ryan. That night was wonderful and the next couple of weeks as well. I shared a great deal with him about how I felt and how I had held back. We told each other that we loved one another, though him first of course. We even made love once or twice, I could tell that it was different. No matter how much I do love Ryan we are so very different. We do not think the same or perceive the same. It was horrible hurting him, telling him that we can't see each other anymore. I cried all night. He will always be in my heart. We learned so much from each other and I do wish him the best.

Of course things happen for a reason, and this goes along with what I am reading at this time – "The Celestine Prophecy". They very next night, Dec 2nd, I met Rob at this 70s party that I was in controversy over attending, first Iowa and now Pittsburgh. I don't know what will happen but there are not coincidences and that whole weekend is full of them.

Anyway, it is so strange that I have somehow become very attractive to the opposite sex. It is amazing, I have finally reached a point where I enjoy focusing on myself. I enjoy reading and reflecting. With this position, however, I become attractive to not only the opposite sex, but to all people. I meet someone, a guy, literally almost every time I go out. It's been about three weeks now that I have been single and I have met three guys whom all have called me. I am not saying that I am interested in any of these people, yet, I find it amusing. It is all about the energy that one exudes. In college I was always desperate for love and now that I don't really care, of course they all want me, how ironic. I suppose people like a challenge. When I think about this I almost want to cry because it is okay for me to be alone. Today is Christmas eve and it doesn't bother me to be alone at all. There are so many things that I want to do with this alone time. I want to:

Write in my journal – ha ha
Read my books
Draw
Play with my new tarot cards

Read some more

Organize my pictures – and the rest of my life, ha ha ha –
of course this comes last for the OTHER

Anyway, I wonder if I will ever find anyone who is intellectually, philosophically, and physically stimulating as well as humorous and intriguing. I must mention that Rob referred to me as intriguing, which I love. He has great word choice, yet, I am concerned that he is not masculine enough. Since there are no coincidences I must go with the flow.

I know that I have a problem forgetting the past. I do appreciate my past, however, for making me the person that I am today. If it wasn't for all the struggles, and the turmoil, and the pain, and even the ugliness I would have never developed the way that I have. I know why things happen the way that they did. There are no coincidences.

I realize that I am different every day. I am not jealous of the rich because they lack personality and character that is built from struggle. I am not jealous of the beautiful because they are only ever appreciated for what appears on the outside. I am very lucky though, and Brooke has reminded me of this, that we are intelligent and beautiful. These have both come with time. I was very much the ugly duckling, this benefits me so that I don't take for granted the way that I look now, I relish in it. I am not mean or condescending towards people. Those many years filled with grief and insecurity have developed my character. When you cannot rely on your appearance you must become attractive to people in other aspects. I have always relied on humor and still do. I love to make people laugh and to make myself laugh at the same time.

Men amaze me. Anyone between 15 and 60 will give me a gaze while I am shopping at the mall. It is fascinating. I am attractive, yet, not perfect by any means. What I posses that draws most of my attention is my height. At 5'9" I do look somewhat model-esk. I never hated my height because I do like the attention.

Well that was my ego boost for today – I had to tell someone. Balance – everything will balance, I am positive of that.

February 4, 2001

Do people ever do what they really want? Are we so torn between what we are supposed to do and what we really, actually want to do that actions are never true? I am torn. I don't know what to feel or how I feel, or how I am supposed to feel? Do they become bad when others are made aware of them? There is the choice of not to tell anyone of your actions, yet, there remains that other person, that person who also partook in the action that makes it real. The other cannot be controlled, all is lost.

Sex, sexuality, lust, fornication, desire, need and want. I want, I want most of all. I want those that are unattainable. I want to conquer to win to overcome. I want pleasure in this remedial world.

The methodical, the controller, the one I will never attain, which makes him all the more desirable. I wanted him, I always wanted him since I have met him when I was so young, so naïve, I knew it was inevitable. I knew I would succumb. When the day was right, when my mind was right, when I had done all that I needed to do. I could say that I knew this was going to happen but I didn't. I had no idea what was going to happen. It is so strange how you can never really know what you are going to do. Perhaps people control their actions and that is how they know what they are going to do, however, this is not true, I am true.

April 2, 2001

Where shall I begin. Of course, the carjacker. He foolishly assumed that I was a "normal" passive female. To his utter surprise I was a 6'9" black male with aggression problems masked by the outward appearance of a white, prissy, female. In all, I saved the car, I won, he lost.

Also, there was Derrick. Derrick himself also masked his appearance. Little did I realize that D.S. actually stood for Dip Shit – literally. At first he seemed very knowledgeable and coherent of his surroundings. He was well spoken and engaged in conversation easily and freely being 11 years my senior. He actually was clueless to his environment. He has absolutely no idea what he is doing, where he is going, and where he had been. Though, it is amusing now to recall his absurd behavior. Although somewhat frustrating at the time, no real damage was done. I now have gained the experience and knowledge to better read the predictable signs of future Dip Shit's:

1) Complex look appears on face when questioned about feelings and/or emotions – hmmm?
2) Previous girlfriend is extremely unattractive and given names such as "leather face"
3) Extreme sexual preoccupation, yet, only with self
4) Dislike of all fatty food? Huh?

Derrick will be much better served by those less attractive, uneducated, and unaccomplished females. More power to him.

Now there comes my Birthday, the most miraculous day of the year. I have turned 23 – wow, I am old, completely an adult, no more college age years left. It was incredible. By far, the best birthday I have ever had. The whole weekend, each day, was spectacular.

Friday I met Jack. It was like a dream, a scene from a movie. Something that is so idealistic that you would never think it to actually happen. It did – someone pinch me.

May 2, 2001

What can I say, Jack? He is just so appealing. He is the picture of a man I had in my mind since I was a little girl - tall, handsome, brown hair, blue eyes, and aloof. The key is aloof. He has it. He is there. He knows. Not everyone knows, but he does. In our world people (not all, just most) are pawns to be toyed with.

This past weekend I watched him and his responses to people. He was friendly and charming to everyone, yet, with me, with a little distance from other people, I saw the cruelty. The same cruelty in which I posses and cannot hide. It is amazing. Generally I am a nice person I believe, however, I know there is something, I have a deviant side that is suppressed. I know he does as well. He mentions things, slight clues intentionally to draw me along, to present enough information that I crave more – clever boy! There is something about him, I have to know his deviant nature that he exclaims is so hidden and only appears every so often. I question what this deviance is; it is not sexual or psychotic killer instincts, so I am baffled? What other deviant things could there be? I am baffled.

I have never met a man that has such a dynamic nature. There are so many things about him that amaze me. Simply put, he is not simple. The way he was at the party, I was the only person he was real to. The way that when he would get up to get something he would glance over at me and hold my stare for just a little longer than I had expected, that's our connection, we know what no one else knows!

May 13, 2001

Is it possible to be so drawn, yet, so resistant to someone at the same time. I have never felt this way my entire life. I think about him all the time. I can't wait to touch him, to see him, to kiss him. At the same time he frightens me more than anyone I have ever known. I would not be prepared if one day he stopped talking to me. This is what I fear. This is what keeps me resistant. I have never needed anyone in my life. I have never been in love and I am so confused right now. I am absolutely terrified, yet, I crave more and more.

May 30, 2001

Perhaps my pessimism in life is directly related to my expectations of others. I have extremely high expectations of everyone and everything and I become extremely judgmental of people who do not meet up to my expectations. I preach this great open mindedness and I do not posses this myself? Am I completely contradicting myself? In this process, this forever long process of developing my beliefs and perceptions of myself and the world around me, am I contradictory? Well of course, things are all still in theory, nothing proven.

Sometimes I feel so confused. I say things that I don't really mean or that I wish I would mean. In a way, however, I don't wish because most of the things I say have to do with emotion, and if I didn't feel those things I wished I didn't then I would be a very cold and uncaring person. Protection, it is all for protection, never wanting to be hurt.

Could I be hurt? I am not sure. There are not many critical statements that someone could say to me that I haven't already thought or stated to myself.

Love, what is love? I have never been in love and I know that because I question the definition, as in how do you know when you are in love? I love everything. Nature is beautiful, the moon at night is beautiful.

I need to fully appreciate the things that I have. I need to stop forever wanting more, wanting perfection. There are different levels in life and at each level realizations are made to the degree that people who were previously thought to be crazy and/or ridiculous become understood. This is very awakening and terrifying because you then must consider all of your current thoughts to be, perhaps, in transition. Therefore, as new levels are reached and new beliefs are formed there is constantly the threat that these beliefs are again incorrect and when the next realization or new level is reached all will again be shifted. Stability never exists unless there is a conscious effort to stop learning. Perhaps this is a rational choice of those who partake because they cannot handle the constant threat of fluctuation that coincides with gaining knowledge. However, when knowledge is not pursued nothing is gained and life is then still and stable becoming monotonous and unliberating. Therefore, my quest for stability will never be achieved by my own definition of what stability entails that I am forever insatiable for knowledge, therefore, leaving me forever unstable.

June 17, 2001

Complexity, I strive for it unknowingly. I create my own controversy. I prolong things in order to appease my idealistic mind, for which it will never be fulfilled. The knowledge that I seek I will never have. Things turn out so bizarrely than what I had planned or believed. This is very confusing.

The past is a tough thing for me. I cannot forget the people of my past. I don't think I will ever put behind me the experience of Jack. There was no closure. Us both being as stubborn as we are neither will forfeit. The breakup stated by me, threw the roommate, telling him not to call me anymore. He did what I said, no call. Not even an attempt to salvage me. Do I think he wants me to leave – no, will he call – no, he is me, I know how he thinks. We are so similar, yet, so different – on totally different plans. I have the idealistic belief that someday, perhaps years from now Jack will realize how wonderful and unique I really am, he will find me. This is what I would like to believe for now. I can't stop thinking about what the psychic said. That I would meet someone in the Spring and then marry him four years later. I cannot devalue the importance that his mother died on my birthday (from cancer) and that her name was Mary. These things haunt my mind. If this does not signify something then I don't know what to think of the world. How can these synchronicities be meaningless?

July 29, 2001

I forfeited. Due to Tim, one date with him and I could no longer tolerate the unknowingness. I emailed Jack, only a few lines with no implications. He responded, to my surprise, with an elaborate explanation of his actions and thoughts. He apologized. I read the email at least 50 times and could not concentrate on anything. I called him, he called back and we talked just one day short of six weeks from that night, eight weeks exactly from when we had seen each other last.

August 13, 2001

Too much. There is entirely too much going on right now. Jack is coming over. The Dr. called tonight and told me that I possibly have the first stage of cervical cancer. Before that Tim called. Yesterday, I went on my first date with Joe. Tomorrow I am meeting with a professor to discuss graduate school.

Cancer is a very scary world. Once it is stated everything else becomes fuzzy. Flashes of chemotherapy and bald heads fill your mind. Cancer is so unpredictable, can show up anywhere, anytime. I am frightened. They say everything will be fine, but cancer has already been stated.

There was a time in my life when I was desperate for men to talk to me, to want me. Now, there are too many. I try and be a nice person. I try to give people the benefit of the doubt, but I am not sure that I should. I thought everything would be easy now, less complicated and convoluted. No, not true. It was easier when I was young, all decisions made for me, now I have to make them.

Jack is here knocking – have to go

August 18, 2001

Friends, I have, by now, told all the male suitors that I just want to be friends. I am not sure what that entails, but I know for Jack it entails everything. I cannot resist his touch, his kiss. Everything just feels so right. In my head thing are not as I want them. But I have that feeling. It's like a high – he makes me high on the euphoria of passion. He even said on the phone this week that our first kiss, each time we see each other, is so intense. He is exactly right. As soon as I distance myself he pulls closer. He emailed, called, and plans for next week, all this from saying that I want to be just friends He said that Drew (his brother) thinks we love each other. Do we? I find myself unable to be attracted to other people. Is this why? Do I love him in some bizarre way? He tells me how he has passed up opportunities, how he has rid himself of the current female suitors. He doesn't want anything serious; he doesn't want to feel liable, to have to consider someone. He says all these things that should make me not want him. I should be rational and understand that we won't be together in the way that I imagine. I don't want anyone else to kiss me. I want him to kiss me. I have felt the intense passion I feel with him. He doesn't want to hurt me. I know, but still he can't take me out of his life and I can't take him out of mine. What will be of us?

August 27, 2001

Saw Jack this past Saturday. I love his touch; I love it when he stares at me. I love how when he kisses me and touches me it is like he can read my mind. He can make me so high, yet, so low as well. Nothing significant happened. I just can no longer pretend that something is not missing. Friends entailed seeing him, I knew that. I knew that we would not be capable of resisting each other. I cannot sleep with someone that I have told we would be friends.

Also something else happened this past summer at UC by the Sea. I was there with Anna and Susan and the other sorority girls and we were drinking. Killer was there, I think he is a lifeguard at the shore every summer, and he had a girl crying next to him the whole night at the bar yelling at him; I looked over at him from across the bar and he didn't look too happy about it.

Another girl told me that apparently he had taken her virginity and he wasn't as emotional about it as she was.

He was there, the guy that had kept me up all night before graduation. Here he was all disappointed in me, I could tell from afar that he had built something all up in his head and he was not pleased (*well, I did have a broken nose from the carjacking that wasn't properly fixed and I looked very different in pictures than I usually look - this gets fixed before grad school in 2002*). Interestingly, there was an older man at the bar, Steve, who was actually owned a house in philly and he was just there on vacation. He came over to me and offered to buy me a drink and I asked why and he said "clearly you are the prettiest and most popular girl here, everyone is always around you and talking to you." I guess he didn't see what I looked like before so he didn't really know how different I looked. Maybe people just see whatever they are and I just reflect how they feel about themselves.

So I started dating this guy, Steve, when we got back to philly. He lived in Manayunk and he had me come to his house and he made me dinner. I was really into him at first because he was about 10 years older and he had his own home but then when we starting kissing and becoming sexual he got really weird. He was very detached about the whole process and he wanted me to do a lot of things in front of him while he watched me. It didn't feel right to me the way he wanted to watch me, rather than feel me, and I felt like there was something off about him. He called me after this encounter and tried to tell me that I was sexually impure or something nuts and he just kept saying all these really bad things about my sexuality. It was as if he wanted me to agree to the sexual labels he was placing on me so that he could mess up my self esteem and get me to do what he wanted sexually. He was really clever and tricky with his psychology and I felt like he was dark and manipulative so I told him that it wasn't going to work out for him. It wasn't easy, he really start to mess me up because he was so powerful and confident that he would not stop because he wasn't getting to control me sexually like he wanted.

September 17, 2001

I have made a decision today. I am going to kill myself if I have a positive diagnosis of hpv. Yes, it seems irrational; I realize how others would say this. But it is not if you knew me. I am incapable of handling sexual defectiveness, for which that is what I see it as. I sexualize everything. There is only sexuality to me. Everything else is a derivative of sexual. It is everything to me. It is raw beauty, it is the never ending field of daisies, it is my constant driven search for beauty, power, and control. Although I have never experienced sex the way that I should have, I can still see the beauty. The passion released, the beast, the darkness. My entire life revolves around sexuality. If the sexuality were taken the beauty would cease to exist. The dream of perfect feverish love gone. That is and only is what I live for. Nothing else compares to this dream. If what I fear were true, the dream would be gone and life no longer worth living.

I cannot engulf myself with sexuality as I do if I am then reminded of my defectiveness. I was told that people are only given what they can handle. I cannot handle this feared outcome. It is not a mere virus to me, yet, a mentally fixating slow death of my beauty, of my passion. Hindrance becomes the death. An imperfection to this degree is unacceptable.

I am prepared to die. I have righted all my wrongs, shared experiences, thoughts, moments, and emotions. I do wish that I could have experienced love to the fullest degree. However, if this fate be true that will not be possible even when I were to continue life. I know myself better than anyone. I cannot bear being permanently defective. I cannot aspire and love knowing the defectiveness of myself.

When fate has been deemed true, I will die quietly alone. No one will know. The calmness of pain killers will drift me into my freedom. This is my fault and I will make it right.

September 28, 2001

Something is wrong, I can feel it. I have felt it for a while now, but it is exceptionally strong tonight. Everything is off, everything looks different. My apparent falsehoods have vanished all the sudden, for no reason that I can determine. It is as if I have sobered from a drunken state to realize the horrors and face them, yet, again. I see everything, all my actions as a façade, a bravado of my will. Is how I behave what I really want? Can someone train themselves to become a new person, or do they train themselves to deceive and lie about their true feelings, about themselves to themselves. How do I feel, I am not sure, it changes constantly. Sometimes, I want people to die, "innocent" people, I don't care, I want terror and pain and other times I want joy and charity and helpfulness. Which is true? Are they both true states? The first seems more real to me because it is raw, it is want that is not intended, hate for all, no discrimination. The second offers a hedonistic view of how the world plausibly occurs. Charity is the masturbation for the lay man, for charity causes instant gratification and pleasure, it has no harm on others, a hedonistic dream. Being "good" causes people to feel good, yet, is this feeling correct or just a masking of the true patheticness that everyone secretly endures in their own mentally insignificant and consciously diminished states. Do people feel obligated toward charity to rid themselves of their wrong or for the mere pleasure. It is never about the other, it is about the self. The goodness done for others is only about one seeking their own pleasure. When a person dies, we are not necessarily grieving their death. They are dead and suffer none. Those left are the ones that suffer. We are grieving our loss, what we want to have back, not their death. Everyone is selfish, some just prefer to indulge in the pleasure of giving, that is their selfishness. Some see past this and do even attempt for they realize the ignorance of the act.

October 21, 2001

       Calmness prevails. This past week, no, last weekend, I saw Ken, Jack's roommate. I am glad that I saw him because my perception is now changed. Ken professed his belief that Jack is gay. I had always joked and considered this, but not ever thinking it be true, yet, it makes perfect sense. His distance, his confusion, the gestures made toward Ken in a joking manner – really representative of his true feelings. The regression back to the ex-girlfriend living in Chicago, it all makes sense. The woman's deodorant, pastel colors, over sensitivity, and overalls. He hasn't yet realized or accepted his true feelings. He reverts to the girl so far away because that is the perfect/easy set up. All his female relationships never work out because he is looking for his perfect girl. In his mind he believes that he will feel strongly for this perfect girl, he will be able to commit, he just has to find her. When really, these feelings just mask his true wish to be with a man. His adoration for Ken, asking Ken to cuddle with him, provocative jokes and sought kisses. The act in high school (while away at a basketball championship). I wondered why he was so open about that. He throws this in everyone's face, so open about, seeming that it is a joke because of all the women who have come and gone, yet, he must want someone to realize.

       Another part of me, however, does not understand how he could touch me and kiss me the way that he did if he really sought the affection of men? We were both extremely attracted to each other. Am I manly – well in a way yes. I wonder if he will realize or if he will marry and realize years later, ruining lives?

       It makes sense to me. I understand now why he found me defective, why he could not commit. All women are defective, yet, I was more attracted to him than anyone, and that is a falsehood because he is not a heterosexual man. He is not what I desire, yet, he was what I desired. I must now rethink what I desire, it surely is not gay men, despite how gentle and sensitive they may be.

November 6, 2001

I feel as though I am going crazy. Everything is so meaningless. I have no focus, it all is a blur, a day to day blur. I cannot stop my mind from thinking. I stare all the times, my thoughts racing through my head, as I look catatonic to the outside world. If they only knew all that I know. Everything is so fast, I want to stop my mind from thinking, from analyzing and fixing. It is too much. No one understands. I am not "normal," but I say what is "normal"? That is merely a perception, a state of mind. Everything is a perception, so what is real, NOTHING, it's all in your head, every last bit. If you weren't there to think of it, it would not exist to you. What do we measure ourselves to, there is no standard, no mold. Everything runs together and I don't care. Men and women are innately homosocial, the bond with each other, they understand each other because they are of the same gender. Men and women do not belong together because they are fundamentally different. Homosexual men get along great with women, usually? Why – yes! Those men who are the most manly men spend all their time with who – men! Social training produces that we are heterosexual – what if children were taught that homosexuality is normal? What would happen then? Men and women unite for that mere physical pleasure when essentially they are to never coincide or understand each other. Perhaps those that become gay or are gay realize this. Genetics, I am not sure?

January 1, 2002

Happy New Year! 2002 has begun. Wow, I feel as though many things have come together for me – all coincide. I wish I had known that all I needed to do was fix myself and everything else followed graciously. I am very content. There is nothing lacking in my life right now. I just wish other people knew how simple it was. Fix yourself, understand your flaws, better your being, and all of your other worries will naturally resolve, almost miraculously.

I never thought that Sean and I would have anything in common. I am glad for my open-mindedness. He is beautiful. He is the kind of person I didn't think existed anymore. He truly does care for me and would do anything for me. I can just see it in the way he looks at me. Sometimes when I think of him I feel as though I am going to cry, not because I am upset, because there is so much emotion that I am overwhelmed. It is so wonderful, yet, so frightening at the same time.

January 6, 2002

I wasn't sure what to do, I wanted to do something, but wasn't sure. My room is too small. I am getting a cold. Tonight was the first snowfall of the evening. The two kitties are lying beside me on my bed. Sean told me tonight that he would still love me if my nose were cut off. We were talking of the movie "Seven" concerning the seven deadly sins. Vanity – am I vain? I have never thought of that, yet, I would not want to live if my nose were missing. I could handle a finger, maybe an arm, but not something to do with my face.

I don't know anything. I really don't know. Everything I want seems not to please me when I have it. I always want more, I am never satisfied.

I can be so many different things, so many different people. Who is really me? I don't know. Am I all these things? Am I a facade? Will I ever figure myself out?

I am just so different. It doesn't work for me. This existence doesn't work for me. I don't want to grow old gracefully, I don't want to be burdened with items and laws and other people's needs. I look at myself and I don't see what other people see. I see hate and paranoia. I see a person that is always thinking of what other people are thinking, contemplating their notion of me. I am wondering what they see when they look at me. I am thinking that their whispers are about me, that they are fake to my face. I consider everyone to have an alternative motive, especially men.

There is so much to think about. So much to put together. I am overwhelmed. My head is too much for me. When I think I am close, that I will finally put it all together, I realize that it is just the beginning again, that I know nothing. There are no definite answers – I need answers. I am restless, I don't know what to do.

What if I can't love other people? What if I innately love myself more than I could love another. Why could I be like this? I don't want to be around another person constantly. I am bored. I am scared for Sean. I am scared that he will be hurt. I don't want to hurt him. He doesn't know me and how I hate. It peaked through this weekend. Almost as if I had waited all this time to be strong enough, as though it were always there, building, preparing for the right day, when I was ready.

-Are the strongest people those with the most self love; the weakest those without self love?

-Does power come from truly knowing you need no one else?

-Does all relate back to sex?

March 3, 2002

Male haunting? Running into someone that was a small part of your past, they are insignificant to you, yet, you are significant to them. I feel bad. I didn't know what to do. Poor Rob. I never explained why I stopped talking to him. Did he reappear so that I can fix what I did wrong. Is there a reason for all chance encounters? I felt so sorry for him. I gave him my email so that I can fix what I had done wrong. He knows about Sean so hopefully he understands that I am not interested in dating him.

March 12, 2002

Sean and I broke up today. I am sad; I will miss him very much. I am sure it was for the best. We are very different; we want different things for the future. I didn't want to, Sean became comfortable to me, but I knew there was something missing. We do love each other, and he was very distraught. We both have our beliefs and they don't suit each other. I love him and I wish the best for him. For bitter sweet sorrow, today I received my letter stating my acceptance into the Ph.D. program for Sociology.

April 14, 2002

I had a dream the other night. I was living in a farm house with Sean. It was on an old dirt road with nothing around it. The atmosphere replicated that of a Country Time Lemonade commercial. Everything was so warm and sunny. It was the morning and we were just waking up. Our bedroom was filled with sunlight from two windows, on one the back and the other on the side of the house. The room was scantly furnished, negating that material items were of no worth to us. We awoke, yawning and stretching without a care in the world on our faces. As I awoke I sat up on the bed and looked at the back window. The view seemed to stretch miles. Our back yard appeared to be a half acre or so and then there was a field of sunflowers that were endless in both side directions. Outwardly, a streamline of mountains could be seen at the edge of sight. There were no buildings or people, just land. I turned to Sean and told him to look at the beautiful sunflowers. I said to him that we should pick them and plant sunflowers in our yard around the house. He commented how silly I was and how such little things seem to amuse me. He laughed and agreed that would be a good idea. Everything was just wonderful.

Sean called me a few hours after we broke up. He said that he had thought about it more and he had made a mistake. I knew that he would realize eventually. His stubbornness affected him realizing that love is more important than anything else. I knew that he knew in his heart that he didn't want to leave me.

June 10, 2002

I am currently recovering from my second nasal reconstructive surgery (from carjacking). This one hurt – it hurt a lot more than that last. Hopefully now all my nose related issues will be resolved.

I have realized that my relationship with Sean is very much like my grandparents relationship. Although my grandfather is much more vulnerable without my grandmother than Sean is without me, though this could just be due to the time together comparison. My grandfather is very simple and pretty helpless without his other half. Sean is very simple as well. This simplicity comforts and frightens me at the same time.

I ran into the infamous Jack on Memorial Day weekend. He looked the same and is still in the caddy industry. We talked for a long time about our families and current interests and then we touched on us for a moment or two. I can tell that there is still a lot there – whatever a lot is that is. He asked if I had been to the pub lately since he never sees me there. That indicates to me that he had been looking and wondering (a pleasant smirk arises on my face with this knowledge). He told me a statement that I can feel very much. I explained that I am more able to let my feminine show at this stage in my life. He agreed that that was a hamper to me previously. He stated that I had all this beauty and I would only let it show for such short moments before I pulled back it all back in. I remember him saying it and his arms moved and the look on his face. There is more there – a lot. He mentioned that he will be living down Stone Harbor this summer. I also noted my week long excursion to the same place at the beginning of August. He inquired as to the location of my shore house, yet, I did not know this information. I suspect this will produce another encounter.

July 23, 2002

I am ready. My relationship with Sean ended a month and five days ago. Concerns had been building and through a perpetuated fate all was thrown into the light and I couldn't hide in the dark anymore. His intoxicated self lashed out in unabridged irresponsibility, the striking of two parked cars. Rather than cut his losses and plead guilty he reinforced his lack of care for others and opted for insurance fraud. There was no salvaging. Not only was the irresponsibility shoved in my face, like a spoonful of garbage, but he also attempted to blame me for this ending due to my lack of unconditional love – yeah! Sean needs a nice simple girl with a simple mind to lead a simple life together. No opinions necessary. I have no hard feelings towards Sean, that is just who he was and who he was is not right for me. It was a great experience and I learned a lot about the future person I want to be with.

I feel that breaking up is like jumping into a cold pool. At first it is completely shocking, as if you cannot believe what you have just done. You're somewhat paralyzed by the change and are completely overwhelmed. Although, surprisingly the longer you stay in the pool the more comfortable it become to the point where being in the pool becomes more comfortable than getting out. I am going to take a nice long swim while I am here and only get out when I see a nice warm towel awaiting me.

Five days ago another fate cam into play. I was awarded a research assistantship with the Institute on Disabilities researching social networking. This means a full tuition waiver, a stipend of 12,900 and being published. I rock!

August 25, 2002

I am just so tired. I don't want, or rather, I can't. It has been so hard and long and I am so tired. I won't make it. He needs to find me because I need him.

I never know how I am supposed to act. I just don't know. I feel like I do everything wrong, I cannot tell what people's intentions are. I will never get it right. I always mess everything up. It never works out and I always feel alone.

December 7, 2002

The semester is almost over, one week left. I should have done work all day, but that was not the case. Semester review – there was Patrick. I was with Patrick for about two months. Patrick was not of the passive persuasion, he was very different from anyone I have dated so far. I became infatuated with Patrick. My infatuation ended, yet, his did not. Patrick threw a violent tantrum and that was the end of that. My infatuation with me, with all men, is no more.

Third Journal

December 7, 2002

I am afraid of my mind. I feel life I am losing control, and yet, I feel as though I control everything. I have never known who I am suppose to be, because I can't just be, there is always a necessary what to be. How can there be nothing for me to do today when I have so much to do. My rapacious desire will be my ultimate demise. I will never be satiated. I am now afraid.

There are always others; other thoughts, beliefs, ways, and lives. The others are in my head and there are too many thoughts. I am so oriented on myself, yet, only in relation to others. A distinction is necessary.

I have loved myself more than I have ever loved anyone else. I had a glimpse of what it would be like to fully love another, but it was only a glimpse and it was terrifying. I am not scared anymore. I am ready.

I am different. Recently, something has changed. My outward confidence has increased due to status identifiers that I have conquered. Inside I am confused. I am frightened of myself and what I think. I have realized to an extent that I will never be able to fully understand another, to figure on what will happen, to be prepared for every circumstance. Everything changes to quickly, the rules change in every situation and there are too many perceptions in each situation.

People frighten me. So much is decided and determined by the way that a person looks. The problem is that there is no one way that I look. Everyone sees me differently so how am I supposed to know how others see me. Does it even matter? Or is it just how I see myself? Can I determine the way that I look? It changes so capriciously, how can I decide? Why is this so difficult?

Sometimes I think that people that are institutionalized are the smart ones, a total rejection of society, a realization that the happiest place to be is in their head. A total creation of one's own reality. All needs fulfilled and the creation of a wonderful place by medication. Are we the unfortunate ones left to deal with the anguish of the world?

Does anyone think about me? Wonder where I am, what I am doing or thinking, if I ever think of them? Am I insignificant if no one does?

Is living just acting? Actions in response to a predetermined script, and if so, can your script change? Is change possible, or is it just a conscious suppression of the ill had characteristics so that your act becomes more and more difficult because it is less and less the true you?

It is possible to become what you desire. Mind does conquer all. It has always been a perception. I am her and she is me. I am the girl who leaves, who is obsessed over, who breaks hearts. This is only possible because it had been molded into my script. The comments foreshadowed this current era. Everything was for a reason.

I know now that I am crazy. I know that I am not normal. I had always thought that others were confused or just didn't understand. I know now that I am different. They don't know the power there is in the mind.

I need clarity. I need my nebulous thoughts to fall into place. I know that I am ready.

December 28, 2002

Everything is an act. If you act that way then you are that which you have acted. One can become what they aspire to be simply by acting the part. All is an act; nothing is pure and real because there is too much influence of expectations and past situations.

December 29, 2002

What is it to be mean? Is sarcasm mean? I have always thought so. Sarcasm is a non-consequential way to be mean; a way to criticize through humor. Although, with being mean, it is only mean based on the receivers perception that it is mean – is this really so? Intent also plays a role as well. However, do people allow someone to be mean to them – is this some sort of exploitation of the weak?

I need something to happen and I am not even sure what exactly it is, of course I think, or I am pretty certain the area of which I want something to happen. This area that I am always focused on. Something just feels unsettled and off.

January 1, 2003

No one understands me. I relate to no one. I hate how people assume their own situation is so much worse than anyone else's. I hate most people. I hate their stupidity and their fakeness. I am sad. You are not suppose to look for anything. But if it is missing, how can you help yourself. I feel abandoned. I feel the way I felt in college, the way that I felt growing up. There has to be something more, something better. I feel like I can see it in other people and I am so afraid that I will never have it. I am becoming mean and bitter. My expectations are never met.

January 16, 2003
Motivation needs motivating-

February 2, 2003
I hurt. He said once that he loved me more than life itself. He now said he loved me but we are not right and I need to move on. My antics didn't work, I lost.

I don't like people. I am scared. They make me scared and hurt and everything is so hard. I don't trust anyone except Brooke. I trust Brooke – only her.

Something has to change, I need help, I am going to self-destruct. I am different. I don't feel strong anymore. I hate people, I hate and hate and hate.

He left – he just left me. Someone that once loved me so much I could see it in his eyes and he left.

I hate. I push everyone away. I want to be alone – that is all I know how to be. Alone.

I am not strong anymore. I can feel the deterioration. I can feel it coming. I am losing control. I don't know what is real and what is not. I see the people and think what they are saying – I think I hear them, what they are saying – about me. They hate me. They stare at me with hate. I don't understand how I can have so much power and be so demeaned at the same time. Their looks, the men, I see their eyes on me – all the time. Starring. I hate the people. I want to be alone. He used me – how can he love me and use me? I don't believe him. I am afraid of me, I was critical and he hates me.

I am scared, I am so scared. I don't know what to do. Why is there so much pain. It hurts – for so long. It never stops. This aching – it is always there.
May 19, 2003

I have completed my first year of graduate school. I did well, but there is certainly room for improvement. I feel peaceful and at ease, yet, at the same time anxious. I am ready, he will find me. I don't want to hurt anyone because I know how it feels to hurt. I have to do what is best for me and my well being. Surround myself with positive people. I feel bad for thinking of people negatively and comparing people and I wonder if this is natural or I am mean.

June 9, 2003

This weekend was rough. I thought I met my husband on Thursday – he never called back? Then I cried on Friday when he didn't call. Saturday I was verbally attacked by Susan – calling my confidence fake and that I am pathetic. When in actuality this was her own feelings of patheticness projected onto me due to me being the only person to show up to her birthday party. Sunday we had a party – Leigh was a drama queen and had a crying fit in the middle of the party, none of the boys I invited showed up, and I am fairly certain that Elizabeth banged the downstairs neighbor though she convincingly pleaded her innocence displaying her impressive acting abilities. I displayed my own acting abilities when I told her that I believed her. I figured Elizabeth is better off with me in her life than not, she's working as a waitress at La Bec-Fin and she got into the coke scene so she probably came over all coked up.

June 10, 2003

I can't help but replay the actions in my head. I know I said things that I shouldn't have to him, is this a lesson for me? He seemed so sincere when he said that I was the sweetest thing, the cutest….What happened, did he just decide that there was something wrong with me? Was he afraid that I was too right for him? Did he have a girlfriend? Did he loose his cell phone? Did someone die? I haven't met someone I really connected with in so long – maybe even forever and I felt that with him. I feel somewhat, or maybe a lot, focused on this one encounter, but I can't help it. Everything I knew about him was right. He jokingly said that I wouldn't call him – why did he not call back. Maybe it has nothing to do with me, but I still want to know. I was so excited. This past weekend was so depressing. This is not where I want to be, these are not the people I want to be around. Maybe he won't come along until all this changes. All I wanted was him, it seems unfair that I have to wait this long. I don't feel connected to anyone. I go through days, months, with no feeling of belonging to anyone. I am not first to anyone. No one calls me when they want to talk to their other half. Is it just me, alone - I don't want to be alone. I want him to call. I want Jimmy R. to call and I don't understand why he didn't. Where is he – I need him to hold me and love me. What is the plan – I need to know. I can't go through a whole nother year of stress and intellectualism without him. It is so hard alone. Without anyone to look forward to seeing to make me smile. I need him to find me. I watch couples and I watch my close friends and I want that so bad and I have never had that – that feeling of being connected to someone. Of understanding someone and feeling safe. Please find me, I am ready.

June 14, 2003

Bars are bad. They are filled with either despair or the hunters – all are hungry wolves looking for their prey. It is all about sex. I don't like the bar; I feel that even going there is advertising myself for sex. I talked to a very attractive boy last night, his name was Brad and he went to Temple Law. We had a great time chatting and then I watched him leave with a girl who told him that she would have sex with him. He looked at me and shrugged his shoulders knowing how he must have looked to me. He returned alone after a minute and I was elated that he had realized the error of his ways, however, this was momentary and the whore came in looking for him so they left again to go do their deed. Perhaps him returning was a game or maybe he really was trying to not give in to instant gratification. He is sorry today, I am sure of it. In dealing with me there seems to be so much disappointment. Why is this? So that I can appreciate my husband even more? I am so tired I just want to stay home.

June 16, 2003

I swear that my cat Charles has some weird sexual attraction to either me or my scent. Whenever I do some room dancing he starts humping whatever clothing item I had recently left on the floor. It is so bizarre. Then he gives me some weird looks. I am not going to change in front of him anymore. I think he is a reincarnated jerk guy who is a pansy deep down and doesn't want anyone to know about it. The couch urinating tells all.

June 18, 2003

I think I am depressed. How can you tell if you are depressed? Am I depressed or impatient? I don't want to do anything.

August 17, 2003

I smoked three cigarettes tonight. I don't even smoke, I don't even like smoke. I think for most of the time my life is in a cloud of smoke. I live in this clouded reality where I try to believe in people and honesty and fate but eventually the cloud subsides and I get a glimpse of the harsh reality and this reality is so much more bitter and unfulfilling than the one I create in my mind, that I almost consistently sustain except for my mere glimpses. A person can create many things. They can create and recreate who they are, their past, even the experiences can shift and reform into what one wants to remember. Pictures are of happy times, they help to remember what was fun and pleasant.

I recreated myself. I threw out the pictures I didn't like. I feel the power I felt when I was a child. Yet, I feel it more because I am away from all her bitterness. I am so aware that sometimes I can't take it. I have worked so hard for 10 years. I've wanted what I am right now. Any place that I walk into people stare at me, whereas I used to stare at everyone else. I pretend that I don't see them, that I am doing my own thing, but I do see them, I always see them. I watch them now more than I ever did before because I am waiting to see if they will look, when they will look, if I have the power consistently in all environments, all situations. I don't think it should be like this. I wonder what people think of when they look at me. If I have this great, beautiful, smart boyfriend, if my life is so great. I used to think this when I looked. But it is not true for me, it didn't work out.

I put trust in people and believe and it never works out. I am always disappointed and hurt and I just want to be by myself. No one makes me feel secure. I like to keep people distant. I think my life is like the ballet, if you sit too close it ruins the illusion. Kurt said that I was one of the happiest persons that he knew.

December 1, 2003

I realized why everything has happened. All that I have gone through. I realize the power I posses. I have the ability to make everyone around me happy. I know that I can be a leader and advocate. I have to make the world a better place. I know now that things will change and I will begin a new happy and exciting journey. I know that my grandparents are ready for their next journey. I love them and how generous they have always been to me. I know that I have to donate the inheritance to people living with AIDS. I know that the way I feel now I can have a serious impact on this world. I am not an actress, I am not an entertainer. I will become part of the public image and then a leader in the field of medical sociology. I will be healthy and happy, I will get married and have two children. I will always try my best to help others and I will forever be thankful for the wonderful life I have been given.

December 6, 2003

Be positive, even when it is hard, that is the best way.

Seriously, I threw up on my date. Alcohol sucks, however, I neglected to tell any of my friends this information. Maybe he deserved it. Went on a date with the guy who was the pledge master my freshman year. He was my pledge master when the sorority sisters gave us to a fraternity for a weekend and he made me sleep next to him while he fondled me the whole night.

January 12, 2004

Matt is wonderful. He is everything I have ever wanted in one person. He does everything right. I am in love with him and I told him last night while he was sleeping. School starts in two weeks and I am scared. I feel more pressure every semester. At least I will have a master's degree.

January 18, 2004

I have potentially ruined Matt's life. Everything is my fault. I feel like I ruin everything around me. Maybe I am forever cursed to ruin any man's life that gets close to me. It was my phone call that caused Sean to crash into two cars and now it was my actions and ideas that caused Matt to get ticketed for pot. What is wrong with me? I feel like I hurt every man around me. A moment can change everything. I always seem to be okay and I feel guilty. Why can't I protect the men that are with me. I am awful. School starts in one day and I just can't imagine going into all this pressure again, then, combined with the possible knowledge that I ruined someone's future. Do I have a curse on me? I don't understand, I don't want to hurt anyone, I want to love.

March 7, 2004

Something feels wrong. I seem to have everything I want but I don't feel that it is complete. I am afraid that I will always feel like that.

March 22, 2004

Work was such a different experience last year. I loved working with Allison. I hate being involved in work politics and I feel that everything I do is scrutinized. I feel like I mess up everything. I got yelled at today that I had committed to work on Friday and then called out.

May 5, 2004

One day life amazes you, the beauty of unexpected joy. He was there, it was exactly what I created in my mind. Things are going to change because he was there.

August 4, 2004

Three months have passed and everything has changed. Jack returned as I had always imagined and the wrongs that occurred before were corrected. Outwardly I was the person I had always been but was afraid to express. My wondering and contemplation has ended. I fully see now the coward that he has always been. He is in no way close to the man I deserve. He is not even in the same ballpark, actually we are not even playing the same game! He called and left this long message about his feelings for me and at the end he started saying his new phone number to call him and here the message machine timed out right at the end of the phone number cutting off the last two digits. Bet he was all messed up about it and didn't know what to do, probably thought about it for weeks.

As it is sometimes hard I must believe that everything has happened as it is supposed to. This summer has changed me. Jack returned to end my anger towards him and to act as a catalyst to end my relationship with Matt. I am actually amazed at how recent events have fast forwarded me to be in this optimal position. I am alone, truly alone. Though I know I have to experience this position. I must go through an acknowledgement of all that I am. Because things are somewhat stagnant I sometimes obsess over my deepest fears and scold myself for the hurtful things I have done to myself in the past. I then think that this is needed, a phase of harsh judgment before the final phase being "the world." Although I have fears, I do believe that I have a great purpose. I know that if I am blessed with health and love I will have a strength of person that is unmatched. I know that I can make a difference in this world; I see how people can be drawn to me. I have felt a great deal of pain; many types of pain. I fear that the pain will never be over, but I also feel a calm that my life is in two stages. Pain and suffering is the 1st stage to produce knowledge and understanding. The 2nd stage is the application of this knowledge. I know that the second stage is beginning and the first stage is ending. It is happening now and I will be fully in stage two when he comes. My soul mate is near and we will spend the rest of our lives applying the knowledge we have gained to help others. He will understand me in a way that no one else has. I am already in love with him. I see him in my mind all the time. I see the way that he would hold me and comfort me. He is so amazingly strong, yet, at times, he will back down and let me be strong for both of us. I will be in complete awe of him. I already love him so much that when I think about him my heart fills with so much emotion that I begin to cry. I cry because I know that he exists, that he is close and that the pain as I have known will be transformed into a wondrous journey of helping and healing everyone that is willing to listen, and even many who aren't.

I know that it is you. I have always known. I love you and I am ready for you to enter my life. I know that you are ready too. I know that you love me and it is time for our love to be realized.

August 8, 2004

I feel that I have to be perfect in every way to make up for the imperfect conditions that were existent in my mother's life. If I am the best that I can be all her suffering had purpose and meaning.

January 30, 2005

My husband is a wonderful man. He is a man that other men admire and look to for guidance. He is strong and secure and he leads others with his love and natural authority. He loves me with such sincerity that I can see it in his eyes. He envelops me with his embrace as I nuzzle into his chest. He is my protector and other men fear his wrath if they were to ever harm me. He understands all that I have been through and how hard I have had to work to reinvent myself. He touches me with such softness and love that the emotion I feel is overwhelming. He holds me for hours just because he knows how much I need to be held. He has dark thick hair and deep penetrating eyes. He is always the tallest man in the room and everyone cannot help but stare at him. He cares about people and acts out of love and never fear. He is my teacher and I am his pupil. He is my husband and I am his wife.

March 27, 2005

I have begun my late 20s. Twenty seven is a good age, a sexy age. I am old enough to be wise and young enough to look good. It is indeed a ripe age. I have been listening to Sexy Sadie every day, I am addicted to the song. School is burdensome, I often don't do my work and don't put enough effort in. My thoughts always come back to my longing; this ever felt longing for someone special, someone strong, someone caring and affectionate. People say that I shouldn't be so consumed with him, yet, he is all that I yearn for, all that I think about. Love comes before everything, and when you don't have love, you have nothing. Nothing has meaning without love.

August 20, 2005

Yesterday Sarah and I went to a psychic. It was a pleasant reading for both of us. I was told many good things. I am to be engaged in a year and a half and pregnant within 12 months!! The psychic told me that I am strong due to the strong colors of my aura. She said that I had a lot of purple around and my nurturing instincts highlighted, so because of this my energy led her to believe that I am ready for children. I believe her, I have been having many thoughts of having a baby. My body is even changing, becoming more voluptuous and baby ready…ha ha ha. She said that my soul mate is around me, that I have already met him, however, we haven't connected yet (to emphasize the connection she intertwined her fingers). I feel this also, I have been surrounded by men, different men this past summer. Also, when I think of one they seem to know this and attempt to contact me in some way. I am big on patterns and I have tried to figure out if there is a pattern to lead me to my soul mate. Men encountered this summer:

Weston – Leo
Pledge Master – Cancer
Matt – Virgo
Sam – Virgo
Frenchman – Gemini
Josh – Leo
Dalton -?
John – Gemini
Conrad – Scorpio
Kurt – Aries

And of course there is always my thoughts of Ian, since no one has made my body react as he did. The psychic told me to trust my intuition. If I were to do this I would have to consider the strong pull I had to him. Although it seems that we will never be?

Perhaps he is very similar to my soul mate and this is why I had such a strong reaction? The psychic also said that I will end up with the kind of person I expect to be with…hmmmm…what can this imply? Well this is all very exciting – I have met him! This is supposed to happen this winter. I would guess November since this is the month that has begun my first two serious relationships (Sean and Matt). That definitely follows a pattern. Also, another pattern that I have noticed is that I recently have been attracting a very large number of Leo's – I hadn't noticed this before. The psychic said I will be engaged within a year and a half!!

September 25, 2005

Tomorrow I begin taking my preliminary exams. When these exams are over everything will be different. I can finally rest. This past week I have felt so many emotions at one time. I met a man last weekend. A man like I have never met before. He was calm and uplifting. I walked in front of him as he was dancing. He grabbed me so I danced with him. We walked into Rittenhouse Square and sat on a park bench. I told him that the world needs more compassion and that people need to be more sensitive with others. He looked deep into my eyes and kissed me in the moonlight. The moon was pink that night. I remember looking at how incredible it looked while driving home from the mall on 76. It was reddish-orange-pink, I had never seen the moon look like that before. He told me that his brother was schizophrenic, that he made seven figures, that he wrote a poem about Narcissus, that he has the same containers in his fridge, that he gives to charity, that he played dungeons and dragons when he was younger, and that he was actually 40, not 30 as he first stated. He was charming and chivalrous and I was taken by him. We had a little accident in the car and this is when I realized I was in complete awe of him. An older man rear-ended us and he got out calmly, discussed the accident and expressed sincere concern for the older man's well being. I have never been in awe of someone the way I felt watching him in that moment. I spent the beginning of this week on a cloud. Then, midweek, fear and doubt began to settle in. He had not called, how could he have not called. Then I began to view him differently, he became a villainous liar who willfully played games with my mind. He was then cruel and calculating, knowing exactly how to behave and what to say to me. I was hurt, my heart broken, my awe a product of deception and cunning. Today is his birthday, exactly six months from mine. Withstanding emotional battles and psychic counseling, I called him to wish him a happy birthday and I left a pleasant message. I am still uncertain which man he is, a hero or villain, however, since reality is a construction, I choose the reality that he is a hero. I must choose to believe that what I felt was real and not fake and that he was real and not false. It is better to be open and feel love and trust that people are good until you are proven otherwise. I am happy to have had the time we spent together, it was the most romantic night I can remember. Fear will not bring love to me, and it will only push love further away. I trust in the universe and that there are no accidents. What happened was meant to be. I will be with my soul mate soon, I know this, and I know that he will be wonderful.

January 2, 2006

Happy New Year! Well, this year should be an interesting one. I spent this past holiday season resting and cuddling with Conrad. I am not sure of Conrad's purpose in my life (he is 8 years older)...but I know that he is an interesting and mysterious person. With Conrad I tried not to judge and to be detached from expectation. It was a very unique experience.

This year I will spend more time in the woods enjoying and communing with nature. I will turn off the TV and be still and meditate. I will set my desires free into the universe and not attached to any particular outcome. I will enjoy the moment and act toward others with love. I will pray to be a better person and pray for others around me. I will not be fearful of change and I will work hard to be positive.

I will work hard at my academics and take school seriously. This next year is an important year for progress and I enjoyed the needed rest that was given to me these past two months. These past three plus years of school have been hard, but I enjoyed the challenges. I need to keep focused and be diligent.

January 26, 2006

Early this morning around 12:30am Conrad and I had it out. We said the most hurtful things we have ever said to one another. I feel as though I knew this was going to happen earlier in the evening. I had been sad and teary eyed all night. Conrad was supposed to come over and he began playing a waiting game with me, almost to see how much it would take until I became upset. We had just seen each other again on Wednesday after not speaking for two and a half weeks. We had an amazing kiss that day, I could feel it all throughout my body. It was so passionate and full of emotion. I felt how much he missed me. We went out together on Friday and met up with some of his friends at this bar Aspen. I had a great time and I felt really close to Conrad. He made me breakfast the next morning and even cooked another round of turkey bacon for me. Together we watched a special on addiction; I thought that was ironic. Something changed that morning, he made a statement "don't get too attached" but I think that was more of a statement to himself. He was beginning to get attached to me, to have real feelings. I know that he can see my thoughts and I wonder if he saw my desire for him to be more than he is, to be what he was meant to be. He must have. He knew and he was hurt.

When I went to his house he told me that he didn't owe me anything, that I shouldn't have come to his house, that he wasn't committed to me. I told him that he can't just pretend that being with me doesn't mean anything and he said that it didn't mean anything to him. I know that he lied; he would have never emailed me after two weeks of not talking if he didn't care about me. He said this because he wanted me to go, because he doesn't want to have feelings. This is why he sedates himself so much. I fired back out of hurt and anger and I said that I felt sorry for him and that he was pathetic. He shut the door in my face. Within this encounter, I calmly handed him a bag and he took it out of my hand...I think this gesture is so interesting because there still was kindness there. He didn't resist or say he didn't want the bag of this that he had given to me, he just took it gently as I handed it to him. We were always better at physical expressions. Included in the bag was a tooth brush I had wrapped in wrapping paper to give to him as a present when he came over since he always joked about where his tooth brush was, meaning there should be one at my house for him. I wonder if he opened it and what he thought? Even though Conrad has pushed me away so much I care about him deeply. I feel his pain and sadness from the harsh circumstances of his childhood. I want to hug him and hold him and take all of his pain away. I want to tell him that he is special and that I know how it feels to be in pain and to have suffered so much at the hand of parents. He knows that our lifestyles cannot be reconciled, that I would never settle for someone that needed so much freedom, but he also knows how much we care about each other and we will always have feelings for one another.

June 2, 2006

So I had my last day at the SSDL (Social Science Data Library) on Wednesday. I am so happy to be moving on and changing scenery. Conrad has resurfaced. We saw each other on Mother's day...interestingly. I was at a light and he was in his car turning. I ended up seeing him the next night after some emotionally charged text messages. I have a special bond with him. We can act like brother and sister, taunting and teasing each other while at the same time be lovers. We have seen each other four times now, and each time gets better. He has become so romantic. Although he is still secretive like always, building a mystery around himself. I am not sure what is actually happening. I worry that I am being swindled or that he is presenting a false self to draw me close to him. He is extremely psychic, so this just makes his actions harder to read. He has told me things that I have been thinking about…like a girl I knew in college…he asked me about her and I was shocked. When I am with him I feel things I have never felt before. These are good feelings of warmth and adoration. At the same time, however, these feelings are terrifying because I feel more vulnerable and frightened of how I feel. I am trying to stay relaxed, with some good conversation from Anna, though it is difficult. I must remember fate and destiny. I did a tarot reading and the wheel of fortune card appeared for the future. Things are going to change in my favor, so I need to stay relaxed and remember destiny.

(in this period I have a near death experience although it does not get processed fully until "Dream Secrets" and I am pretty sure Conrad tried to poison me through another girl)

August 12, 2006

Summer is coming to an end slowly. Some surprises occurred this summer that actually benefited me greatly. Biocrap turned out to be awful and after two weeks I was unemployed with about 2,200 dollars. I ended up taking on some independent consulting due to circumstantial force that will look great on my resume. Since of the end of June I have not had to work for anyone. This has been the best summer ever. I have been reading my family literature and relaxing. I have also been working on my spirit and focusing on giving out love and joy as much as I can.

Today I went to the pool with Joanna (from high school) at her apartment complex and I had a wonderful afternoon. I read some family text and we chatted about boys. While we were sitting near the pool a pretty orange butterfly came over and sat down next to me near the stairs. I had love in my thoughts and I told Joanna that I wanted to pet the butterfly. I reached over slowly and remained filled with love and I gently pet the butterfly's wings. It was so wonderful that the pretty little butterfly was not afraid of me and it let me pet it!!! Joanna was impressed with the situation as well. Then when we went out to eat a little boy walked by the window and he bend down to look under the shade and he waved at me – like he knew me. It was very sweet and I think being a child the little boy could see my inner love. It was another reminder that my inner love has grown stronger.

Also, a reason I believe that it was necessary for my inner love to grow stronger this summer is because I met Ian. I am not sure what exactly will happen, but I do know there is a strong connection both physically and mentally. We know each other's thoughts without even realizing it – which makes interacting very satisfying and pleasant. I have to remain focused on my love and not allow fear to enter my heart.

August 23, 2007
Well, much has changed! I am spending a great deal of time alone thinking. I don't have a television anymore, but still can watch movies. Some may say that I have become somewhat of an isolationist, but it seems to me that my worldview and my perspective are not shared by many. There were people in my life that hindered me – that did not want me to be my full potential. This is a transitional phase so that I can regain strength that others have absorbed from me. I need to consciously create the situations and experiences that I desire – that benefit my growth. Change is not a problem for me; my mind is strong and can create greatness.

October 13, 2007

Darkness chases me. It has ever since I can remember. Drugs and alcohol allow darkness in. If something has been with you long enough you become used to it, it becomes a comfort and a sense of identity. I can feel when the darkness takes over and by then it is too late. I am no longer in control and my wrath has no limitations.

March 25, 2012

Dear Diary,

Love is here and the darkness has passed. So much has been accomplished. Sitting here in my new living room, turning another year older, it's going to be a wonderful year. I went into the darkness for a while and it was worth it to see what other's have seen. The book is written and I feel so much better. Joseph is my hero, he makes everything fun. We are living together and tonight I was moving some books around in his office. He went to bed in the room upstairs and I found a beautiful shell pendant. It was the same one we saw when we were out with his friend Dan in Manayunk just a few weeks ago. I wonder if he bought it for me for my birthday? He does things like that, he really thinks about what will please me. It is such a delight being with him. Here is a person that really cares about others and wants to help them. He takes care of me and it almost makes me scared because no one has ever taken care of me in this way and what if really I am very crazy and if someone starts caring for me then all the crazy parts will come out because if I can let go and really really release I could be this whole other person. Sometimes I think that I am really this very soft and gentle person that has so much feeling I can't even leave the house because the outside world is so harsh and such terrible things happen. I even remember this movie with a woman who had agoraphobia and couldn't leave her apartment. It was Sigourney Weaver – she was the woman. She may have even had a doctorate or something ridiculously similar to me. I think someone attacked her or something and she just lost it and fell apart. I always looked down on the people that fell apart, you know, how can you expect other people to take care of you, I guess I consider that rude.

Even though I think about it I would never let it happen. I pull through and keep going. Rolled my car three times on Kelly Drive last year, December 1st 2011! Was dating this kid Rob, Jeff's friend that I knew for a few years. He was a mess and a big baby. I was even mad at Jake for letting me date him. Here I was coming out of two year relationship with an alcoholic, Todd, who lied about everything. That was interesting. I think the best part about that whole relationship were the deer! The deer were great!

Conrad still hangs around watching what I am up to. He checks in here and there wanting some lovin'! He's a big baby too, wanting his mama's teat, probably stuck in the oral phase. He is still with me in my thoughts. Sometimes I feel like he is here watching me. Talked to baby scorp on the day of the earthquake. I do love my lover Scorpions for they are so very lustful.

The earthquake shook Josh all up and I tried to help him get on track. Chuck was around too, always trying to get me to be with him. He's still watching me as well – can feel it (remote viewing). The past five years have been such a journey. Now I see that I am more of myself, being far from oneself is hard. Especially when you know you are far from yourself and getting further. Love heals and brings you back; it calms all the hate and changes it into forgiveness. Acceptance of the other is really beautiful and healing. Now that I have a Ph.D. I feel calm and peaceful about the future. It wasn't possible for me to feel like this before, and maybe that is my own fault, however, it works now.

I wonder why I didn't write anything is the past five years? What kind of a writer does that, do I have some other secret journal somewhere that I forgot about and I was actually writing in that journal the entire time? Could be possible, I really don't have the greatest memory. I don't remember lots of things from high school. I was looking through my old papers that I had written and I don't remember writing them at all. It is almost scary. No memory of any of them. I think I only fully remember things that are very emotional. What this means then is that for a long time I was completely disconnected with my emotions -all throughout high school and college. My professor in college remembered this incident (told me when I was an adjunct instructor at Brynell) my freshman year in her class that I had no memory of? Why is so much of my memory gone? Maybe it's better that way. I feel like now I am starting a whole new life and I probably don't need to remember those earlier parts. I understand how everything is connected. In 2008 I moved into a different apartment in Manayunk. I see that my journal writing stopped. There was something dark about that earlier apartment (lived there from 2002 to 2007). I am worried that where I have moved to also has a spirit. I can hear something jumping upstairs at night when Joe is sleeping. I just started hearing it tonight. I will fix the situation. It might be the guy that built this house, Mr. Grant. I am here to heal and will always make it better!

April 6, 2012

Woke up today and remembered this intense dream about Conrad. We were acting like teenagers sneaking around a big house, drunk with love and desire in the summer. So sweet he can feel and so real it seems. He is so darling in the dream, I almost wish he could really be like that or somehow is he really the person in the dream? So soft, he is always so soft and delicious. Wonder what is happening and if he really is changing and becoming his true spiritual self!

Everything feels so different when I am there in a dream. It's this whole other world where a new kind of interaction occurs and I really feel I am somehow interacting with the essence of the person. I know some part of them must be this way in reality. We were coming closer together and Conrad was more open. You know, I thought back and there were other instances that I believe men really did want to be with me and I completely either ignored the whole thing or just messed it up subconsciously because I would have went down a completely different path, a much more loving path, and somehow I wouldn't allow myself to do the "easy" path. Well those relationships are still deserved and will return in the unique way they were always meant to be like a beautiful dream.

April 11, 2012

So, Joe and I watched this movie the other day, it was called "The Resident" and it was this crazy scenario that reminded me of a 'dream' I had back when I lived in Manayunk. I woke up and saw the neighbor guy from upstairs was on my bedroom floor next my bed. His pants were down around his kness and he had an ether soaked pad in his hand. He looked asleep. I woke up in the bed and saw him for a split second and then I woke up again (for real?) and he was gone and everything looked the same. What the fuck was that? Was it real or a dream? After I saw that I made sure to lock the door to my apartment. Sometimes I have these dreams about men and I think I can see their thoughts or intentions or something like that because I have seen some really weird stuff. Men are fucking weirdo's, I mean really, most of them are, but, hey, I guess you need balance and all in the world so you give some lovin'.

When I was finishing my dissertation and I was very sober and meditating a lot I could walk by a man at the supermarket and literally hear his thoughts about me. For real, it was almost too much. I would hear his thoughts (being sober wasn't an option for me for a long time because it was literally too overwhelming to be around other people!). I could always do this to a certain degree but it became so much more clear when I raised my vibration so to speak. One time I walked by a guy in the aisle at Acme and he wanted to beat and rape me, heard it loud and clear. I moved to another aisle very quickly. On the other extreme I could hear my students uniformly on the first day of class when I would walk in, they thought I was pretty. Interestingly, that is what the first judgment is - our appearance. I think we are all psychic to a degree for self survival and protection. The animals are too, if there is a flood they are always the first to move to higher ground!

I had this other dream once about my ex's uncle. He owned a circus, yes, a circus. Well, in the was chasing me with a knife in my dream and he tried to stab me and he actually sliced my upper arm just a tad. Right away I ran up the wall and around in circles. Tricky, eh? Yes, I can run up walls and fly and do all sorts of things in my dreams. He was a scary guy and knowing this was so burdensome because his family didn't even see it at all. I can always see who people really are in my dreams. Can't wait for my new bed. Going to get more focused soon and get some things done.

April 23, 2012

So, I was just taking a sea salt bath and I remembered going on a date with this medical student that lived on city line ave. We went miniature golfing and we ended up in my apartment. He pushed me against the wall and put a knife to my throat and asked me if I was scared. I said no, of course, and he just stopped. Before that he kind of tried to drown me in the bath tub. We got caught in the rain and he said that I should get out of my wet clothes or else I would get sick. So we ended up in the shower. I got in and then all the sudden he got in too. I still had my clothes on. I am sure there were drinks involved. Anyway he tried to drown me for a second then pulled me up and said sorry? WTF, seriously? You know when we were driving to the golf place I knew something was wrong with him. He said he had fish and I asked right away if they were Parana, and he said yes, he had Parana. Should have ended the date right there!

There was this other time that I met this guy at a concert that I ended up going to alone by accident. Lilly Allen – yes, and I met this guy who later I saw had a scar on his lip from having that special surgery. He was an interesting guy and he was the 10th child. He lived in Kensington or some horrible area, but I went anyway because he said he had some pot. This was a later day after the concert, which I got to go backstage cause of this guy and some security guard who made me kiss him or something backstage. Anyway, on the way home one night while I was high I ran into this crazy looking guy near Strawberry Mansion. I might have been right there at the actual mansion. It had a circle drive and a separate building. This guy was carrying what looked like a rolled up rug. Literally, looked like he was carrying a dead body and here I slow down the car to ask him directions. He had a bright pink polo shirt on and I think there was a BMW there. He looked so completely whacked and here I am so out of it my instincts are all f-ed up at 3am. So I roll the window down a little and ask him where 76 was. He grabbed his forehead and pulled what was very little hair he had left back to the middle of his head and was just so whacked looking. I had the doors locked on the car and my guy friend explicitly said to not get out of the car (when I was leaving). So here then the whacked out guy says that there is a woman in the house and that I should go into the house to ask her, he said she would tell me where to go. He lied so calmly and so easily. He thought I was stupid enough to think that there was a woman in the house. He wanted me to get out of the car so he could do something terrible. I looked back pretending like I believed him when he told me that there was a woman in the house, how clever, a woman of course. I told him after looking up that I didn't plan on getting out of the car and then we looked at one another for a minute not sure what the other one was going to do. Then I just drove off. Drove off very quickly. He couldn't do anything. He couldn't do anything because I was in the car and could have called the police so he could not follow me. I was so scared all the way home. I was so scared that he wrote down my license plate and would find me later. That car is gone now so I hope there is no trace. If he ever looked me up he could still know who I am. He was scary, he looked like a very preppy rich kinda guy, with a lot of money and control issues.

So if I started to write down all the dealings I have had with men I think I would need another journal! Ha! So, how do I get all these emotions out? Things have built up for a very long time. Exercise is good, I will focus on that this summer. I want my true self to emerge, the real me, before any of this all started. Who is that by the way? Some archetype someone made up? Who wants some kind of definite reality to proclaim as truth? Maybe? Or maybe not? The true me is probably a lot more complicated than someone who is all light and happy as one would think a true self would be. There is an underlying belief that all is good and while this is wonderful and nice why does this reality ever so present a very different experience. These people "channel" other beings in this magazine called "Sedona" and they say to let go of your ego and all and then I wonder….well, how did they get published in the magazine? There had to be some kind of ego drive or belief that they should be published, correct, or it wouldn't have happened. So the whole thing seems contradictory to me. The ego is connected to confidence and confidence helps to manifest. The ego isn't all bad, is it? We have to have some kind of personal identity to currently function in this society. If we let go of the ego we would have to let go of our whole concept of identity and even language, so what are these people saying? They need to be clearer and if these beings are from another world watching wouldn't they be clearer.

July 7th 2012

Everything is just so intense right now. Joe and I went to see this angel lady on June 11th and she said these intense things to both of us. That I am going to have two children who will be future spiritual leaders (I always knew that – this is why I got the Ph.D., for you, not me). Anyway, I kind of knew – that is another part of my reading, talking with my angels. I am psychic, apparently a very able and gifted psychic. She said that I have a package, so to speak, of abilities and they are gifts that I must use to help people. I am a medium, clairvoyant, and psychic healer and these were given to me by my great grandmother Beulah, who she said was a spiritual powerhouse. She then told Joseph we were going to have the children and they could be twins! This was so intense for me, more than I showed anyone, but really it was.

July 18, 2012

Well, this past week and a half was interesting. Good old Judd (from college) emailed me and said he was looking for me all this time. So romantic, he's a little wacky though, you can never really trust him long term, he just pops in and then pops out. He can't help himself, I think he is drawn to me, my innocence from when we first met. That's why he responded so quickly to my link. But then he realized soon enough just how smart I really am. I can pretend for a while, it is part of me to be naïve, but that is only part and there is the other part that knows there is something off about him. I think he fools everyone, like Jack (who actually visited me around Memorial Day in 2011 – he tried to have some kind of detached sexual encounter, I wanted nothing of it). They are very similar because I was with them both during a very innocent period of my life (well kinda) and they both return to me almost compulsively. They remember the innocence. They are innocence stealers, predators, and now they are both coaches and I am horrified – what do I do, how do I help? No one will listen to me and understand that they just feel wrong. Judd did not have the right reaction to my email. He should have been concerned that someone could be hurting children – he didn't act like that at all. He was terrified and just acted like nothing happened and now he just ignores me. Something is seriously up, maybe they even know each other or something all fucked like that.

At least Joseph is kind and compassionate. He is gentle and understanding. I do feel better knowing that I have a caring partner.

September 13, 2013

So, I had a baby boy! Leo Nathan has arrived as my son! He came on 9/6/13, a Friday morning, it was actually a gorgeous day outside, sunny and beautiful. Labor wasn't even that bad. I had him at home in water and I can't believe that it all went so well. He is so sweet. At first I was scared of that he represented, of the responsibility and the rite of passage into motherhood. Would he be perfect, could I be perfect. How would it all pan out? How could I control everything to make him safe? It was very overwhelming for the first few days. I would cry periodically and exclaim that I was a horrible mother and it was my fault. Joseph would always calm me down and say all the right things to make me feel better. When I look at him I am still overwhelmed. I think of all the bad things that could of happened and the pain that other people go through. How do you make sense of it all? I think about what Brooke said to me over and over – "what if you can never have children" and I just have so much hatred and anger toward her. How could someone say that to anyone? Speaking of which I had a dream last night about those college girls from Brynell– they were all there and were bringing me down. They must have seen Leo's picture that I posted on meetup and are talking about me. What is it with me and women? It just does not seem to work out very well most of the time. It must be because of my family or maybe I just see it as undesirable to connect with women, men have the resources anyway. I emailed my chair at graduate school to let them know that I had a baby and one person emailed me to say congratulations. Are people afraid of me? Oh, whatever, it takes too much time trying to please people that don't really matter anyway. What matters is Leo and Joe (and Tucker) – love that cat, I even have dreams about him!

Leo had his first bath today and I was so happy that he enjoyed it and he seemed to have a nice time. His belly button came off on Friday the 13th! Since then he has been doing tummy time or his gym mat. I can't wait until we can do exercises together and I can move around more. I think Leo is getting bored because all I do is sit around because my vagina feels like it got kicked by a horse in the front if I stand for too long. Other than that things are well.

You know Leo's birth was in the money room of the house (according to feng shui) and I wonder if his birth will somehow become profitable. I think Kat the midwife was impressed with me, however, no one in her online community seems the least bit interested in anything that I post. It doesn't really make sense to me that they post these questions for one another when you can easily look up expert advice online for any baby question.

So, anyway, Leo is a cutie. Of course I would like him to look more like me, but he is very handsome with his Italian look. People do have a great deal of darkness and I am sure that people aren't all happy for me. It's hard when you can see everyone's darkness – the burden of the owl totem! It makes you far more likely to isolate yourself. Most people have some degree of darkness, some have much more. Those that do have more are usually aware, to some degree, that I can sense their darkness. It frightens them because they usually appear so differently to other people. I can always see the truth. It is a blessing and a curse. People are big fakers!

October 1, 2013

Leo is my little man, obviously the relationship is very layered and complex. Last night I could not sleep for three hours as my thoughts keep going to when I was a teenager and the men that were around me. I thought about how I was dating Bobby and how I really did like him. We used to make out in the back of the Buick when I would drive him back to the Knoll school – when it was an all boy private school. They would have these dances that were open to the public so a girlfriend and I would go to the dance. There was so much lust in the air that the air felt wet. I remember when Bobby and I met – he chased me into this other room when there was no one else but us. He kept asking me to dance but I said no over and over. He was very persistent and I finally gave in. When it came time for my senior prom I asked Bobby and he said he couldn't go because he was leaving the day before to go back home. He said that the ticket was already purchased and there was no way to change it.

My heart was broken and I told my mother how he wouldn't change plans to go with me. My mother said it was his mother that didn't want him to go with me so she made sure that he wouldn't be able to. She told me that his mother didn't want him to be with me. I guess I was some kind of townie girl to her like in "An Officer and a Gentleman" That I was trouble or something. It should have been that we went to my prom and had sex afterward. That was the natural progression and it was normal and healthy.

Bobby called my home the next school year but I was so angry at him by then since I had to go to my prom with someone I didn't really care about. It was a ritual that didn't get fulfilled. He tried when he got back in town but it was too late. I was in college by then and everything had changed. I had sex with someone else and he should have stood up to his mother. I didn't want to be with him anymore.

There were a lot of men around me when I was young even though I think of myself as not being very popular in high school. When I think about it my identity at this time was very unsure. Thinking back to it I am still unsure of who I was to anyone. I present a rather bleak image but maybe it really wasn't the way I used to think it was? I know I told myself a not so good narrative about who I was and I know that I was never fulfilled, I wanted more, I wanted the story to be better.

When I was a sophomore in high school I went to the harvest ball with my friend Lilly's brother, who was a senior. He was into me but I didn't really care, I thought I could do better, be with someone better or something like that. He was very nice to me but I don't think we really had anything in common. I ended up becoming obsessed with this guy Howie – yeah really! I would think about him all the time. This girl Katlyn at lunch was seeing him before and she was the first to tell me about him. He had this long hair to his chin. So after like months of thinking about him he ended up asking me to be his girlfriend. I can't even remember the events that led up to it but I do know that him and Lilly's brother were friends. We were sitting in his basement or someone's basement and Lilly's brother, Jake, left. Howie had just asked me to be his girlfriend and then he was trying to make out with me and I got really nervous because I had only ever kissed two other people so I wasn't sure what to do. I kept saying no, that I wasn't ready because I was so shy. So then he dumps me. I think I was his girlfriend for maybe less than a day. I couldn't believe that he could have been so cold and changed so fast. It scared me on so many levels and made sexuality even more complicated for me.

Honestly, sometimes I wish I would have drank some alcohol in high school so I could have been relaxed and felt more outgoing when I was with guys, but I don't know how that would have worked because I was never allowed to go anywhere. The one time I did make out to a party in the woods I had to leave almost as soon as I got there because it started so late. The first time I drank alcohol that summer after high school it ended up being all out-of-control because I was so suppressed. My mother saw Jason at the town Fun Days when she was selling tye dye t-shirts. She told him to call me because I think she had a crush on him. So I ended up dating Jason, who called me right after prom.

Well, he was not very aggressive sexually, maybe because his parents were always in the next room and they were really into church, but this one time when they were away and we drank alcohol he got really aggressive. It was his friend Kevin that instigated the whole threesome. This Kevin guy went down on me with Jason there and I don't even know how this could happen. Jason is standing next to me with his dick out and Kevin is between my knees? So then here Jason the virgin all the sudden wants to have sex with me when he was saving himself. The worst part is that I was suppose to go with Jason to a party at Kevin's house and Jason calls me to say that I can't go because Kevin is not comfortable with me being there at his house since he has a girlfriend. He tells me this on the one right in front of my uncle, because they were visiting at the time, which was so embarrassing. I had told everyone that I was going to this party and now I was dis-invited. Jason, of course, was still going to the party without me because I asked him. Now see if I had been with Bobby this whole thing would have been avoided. My mother picked out an asshole for me and didn't even know it and Bobby's mother ruined our relationship.

October 12, 2013

Today I was so in love with Leo in this one moment I started to cry. The way he looked into my eyes was so overwhelming emotionally. Right before he smiled at me, what seemed to be on purpose. He is so little and helpless, so vulnerable. Now everything is different. I realize how connected we really are to everyone. Every person out there is someone's child and they were subject to whatever the emotional state of the mother was during childhood. It is all the mother – she creates everything. Leo is so good and he was so fun tonight when we were doing his stretches on my lap. He loves looking at me and it feels so good to just gaze at each other. Today he was wearing a 6 month old outfit, he is growing so fast.

October 17, 2013

Today was our last appointment with Kate our midwife and it was a really nice visit. Tyler, the assistant, said that I make beautiful babies! It was a good time. They both loved seeing Leo and said how big he was, weighing 12.55lbs! He is already wearing 6 month size clothing. Leo is such a lovely baby, he is 6 weeks old and everyone loves him!

October 25th, 2013

Finally, I am healing. It has taken a while for me to even start to feel like my old body again. Everything got shifted and seems to be returning into position. A few days ago on 10/21, Leo said his first word – milk- it was clearly milk and today when I was combing/brushing his hair he said "that's good."

October 27, 2013

Today was full of many ups and downs. We tried to go to Merrymead farm and buy some pumpkins with Leo but that turned into a whole ordeal since I was in pain and we forgot the thick blanket. It was cold and there were so many people in line outside. It felt horrible and this was supposed to be fun. I went there before with Heather and it was fun. This time was different. I was looking around at all the women and children, the families, and wondered how they do this everyday! I saw joy and suffering mixed all together at the harvest fest. I wondered how all these women with children dealt with healing after giving birth and why no one told me what to do to heal after the birth. Don't remember this being covered anywhere and it is so important. Nobody ever tells me anything, I always have to figure it out, fumbling along in the dark. I spent so many years trying to help guide people and still no one guides me. No one helps me along, that is what it feels like. Is that really the case or do I just remain stuck in an old feeling that isn't the truth anymore?

October 30, 2013

Leo loves standing tall on his feet on mommy. He was so cute tonight. Everything always seems better at night. Today was rough, got a little sad thinking about how much I was neglected as a child. I think about Leo and how much I want to do for him. I want his life to be easy and full of love. He will feel wanted and loved and supported always. He will get it all. In the midst of my sadness there was a knock at the front door and then the doorbell. I had to stop breastfeeding to answer and it was this guy Sal running for borough council. He nice and naïve, I thought I could do this, I could be a council member. Had my eye on Secretary of Health and Human Services for a while now, guess I need to start somewhere! Speaking of politics I saw online that Laura from college got married. She really is a nice girl, but a little naïve as well, I mean she is a republican for goodness sake and she isn't a millionaire – WTF, ha ha ha. Those girls from college piss me off, none of them were even really my friend. They certainly are not happy for my success at all. I don't know if I was really that bad in college or if they are big phonies. I could be a little of both. They still have their little cliques and keep in touch and I tried this for a long time with a few of them but it didn't work out. Maybe I changed too much, too far from where they are, that is scary to them. Here I try to connect and sometimes there is a response, but others have been cold. I wonder if it is because I didn't get married and they did and now they are trapped – my worst fear. This journal is from Lynn from college and I have used it all these years even though I hate how small it is and how hard it is to write and these little pages. I wish that people were more thoughtful and more caring.

I am stunned when I reach out to people and they don't respond. No one congratulated me on getting a Ph.D., everyone is just fucked up mostly. If you're not fucked up you probably will find it hard to have friends, people don't like those who have it together, no one to complain with them and suffer, and be the victim. Yeah, it's your fault if you life sucks, that's right! They just used me in college, like some kind of jester to entertain. I wasn't sure of who I was back then and I allowed these women to somewhat take advantage of my flaws. No one told me how to get it together or try to understand why I upset or why I got so angry when I drank. As long as it was fun for them or whatever. They don't really care about me, but Laura seemed genuine when we were really young. She was real and nice. I think the other girls corrupted her or got her to see me in a different light. Brooke is pure evil, I now understand why this one fraternity called her Zool. She is very manipulative and controlling, but not more so than my ability and that really frightens her, she can't control me. I bet my whole asshole problems are coming from them. Talking about me and gossiping. I can feel that kind of stuff, it physically hurts me. No love at all. It was only after they were out of my life that I was able to move onward to have a family, a child. I guess none of them saw me as a mother. We'll see what happens as the news spreads. I sent Laura an email so I know they know, at least half of them. What a waste of my time and money being the maid of honor in those two weddings and trying to be such a good friend when I could. Sitting at that baby shower and having none of them speak to me or even look at me, Laura included, that made no sense. Fuckem. I am moving on and moving up. I got the sparkle!

October 30, 2013

I am so angry at Brooke for what she said to me all these years. Always telling me "what if you can't have children" – seriously, what the fuck is wrong with her. Who says that over and over. It started when she was pregnant with Elle. And that whole "single forever" picture frame. Even Brad said that was mean. I don't get it, maybe she didn't want to be friends with me anymore. She only liked me when I was a mess, made her feel better about herself or something whacked! Giving me that book about women being bad ("When She Was Bad"). Yup – she wanted me to be the bad girl so she could be the good girl. Well, that is just too simple for me. So here my mother overheard Leo and found out that I had a baby. She called me later that night and then started talking about her dogs. For real, you would think that she would care that I had a baby! I mean, really cared. No one cares, not really. I used to care, maybe, but maybe now I don't care either. I cared about all these people that didn't really care about me. Not a good pattern, but it was imposed on me at a young age. That is what I must think of the world, that no one really cares, that must be how I felt as a child and still subconsciously I attract these experiences. Joseph cares though, not sure why, but he does in surprising ways. Could be that he is trying to isolate me by getting rid of all my college friends or could be a very beneficial cleansing. I didn't really think about how much I got back from them (especially Brooke and Erin) until he pointed it out. He kept saying "what do they do for you?"Aria is a good friend, she does care and I think she has genuine feeling which is important. Some people do a lot of emotion work and lie to themselves about all the stuff they have created. Hell, even I do it sometimes, but not too much, don't want to get too far off from what is true. College was a time when I was forced to live with other women and befriend them. Socially, it was very gender segregated.

November 1, 2011

Yesterday was a fun day. Leo said mamma for sure, I heard it. Today, actually, this evening has been very tough. I feel like a horrible mom, he was so upset and I was upset because he was so upset. I feel bad that his skin is not perfect. It is all my fault, like I already ruined his life. Here my mother was awful but I didn't have any rashes on my face so I guess I am a worse mother than her. I want to fix it and I want him to be adored. I feel like everyone just acts nice about it when they really think I am a failure. I can't go to the party tomorrow because I can't deal with all the pretending, like everything is ok and I am not a failure when I am. You know I read back to things I had written before and I used to have so much hope about the future. It seems like the future is here and It is not like I had imagined. Did I mess everything up? Leo was hysterical tonight.

I want to be a really good mom. To present myself with grace and charm. Leo can feel my emotions and he will then reflect those emotions in his appearance. I need to be more secure in my appearance. All those years of trauma have really done a number on me. It must be that I don't think I deserve a baby with perfect skin. Why do I have to punish myself, think that I don't deserve the best. Do I deserve the best, am I my best self? Katie was here today and I blame her somewhat for the crying for me and Leo. There is something dark about her, I had that dream that she was on heroin – strange. How do I include more joy in my life? Katie is depressed like me. Everyone around me is probably depressed like me (or else how would they be attracted into my life?). She basically told me that looks don't matter, yet, don't pass your insecurity in your appearance onto Leo. I get the insecurity part but looks do matter. They can define your whole life and will for many. Every day feels like a roller coaster. It's all over the place. Leo's face changes every day and it depends on how relaxed he is, so when he cries I know it is not helping his face and I feel even worse. I try to be positive but I don't feel like I am always my best self. In fact, I hate who I have become a lot of the time. I feel like it all is not really me. I took a wrong turn somewhere and got lost on a long road. I should be thankful for all that I have but I wanted so much more for myself. I wanted to be grand and to be the best mother and friend and lover. I don't have passion anymore; my heart is broken from too much pain. Now I just expect pain and I can't stop expecting pain so it is always there, waiting.

Second Journal – started writing in again

November 6, 2013

My new truth is that I am a mother. I let things go and have a very free spirit. I love my baby boy! He is two months old today. It looks like I took a long journey to the dark side and came out a shaman! Everything is getting better. A new narrative is forming. There is more love and joy. Leo has brought a great deal of joy to me. I love when he smiles at me and coo's. He is so full of love and innocence. I am now part of the cycle of life, a true member, a mother and lover.

November 7, 2013

My mother took all the joy out of my childhood. I realize now it began so early, even in utero. She continues to try and put this energy on me. I won't let her do this anymore, but how do I not let her do it? She does it every time I speak to her and I would have to stop speaking to her. She makes these intense judgments of everything I do, of whether or not God loves me and I can't stand it anymore. I've tried to help her and tried to create boundaries but she doesn't care. She only thinks of her needs and no one else. Well good thing I know exactly what not to be as a mother. Nothing was ever fun with her, it was always miserable and depressing and full of fear and who wants to live like that. Other people have started to show me that people can bring positivity to you. Aria, Kat, and even Joe's dad have all said really healing things to me about Leo and about me as his mother.

I have my own child now and I don't want to have to be her mother anymore. Both of them, my grandmother and mother, call me to tell me all their problems which seems to be the reverse of how it should be. So here are two women that never supported me emotionally, yet, expect full emotional support from me whenever something happens in their life. So am I supposed to forgive, ok, but then what? Do we still talk, I hate talking with either one of them. They are both full of pain and it's not my pain to deal with. It was all started with Beulah dying in childbirth (my great grandmother). She died and there was no mother. I had Leo the right way, the way it should have been for Beulah, with a midwife, with caring women around me. Will they both realize that the cycle of pain is over, that we are not going to rehash the same old fight about mothering over and over again. There are two messages on my phone that I don't even want to listen to because it is always so depressing. I want family members that are happy for me and who see me as someone that has done great things with her life, as someone who is good and wants to help others, as someone who is kind and loving. I want Leo to see me this way and I am happy to let him be the child and to enjoy this time when he is learning who he is and the ways of the world. He will be free of any of those types of interactions that I experienced over and over in my childhood. My mother even told me how I had these skin problems when I was an infant and look how that has impacted me all my life. I had a reoccurring dream that I was terrified to be in public without makeup. That is some serious deep down stuff that was hammered into me, over and over, in my early days. Well, no more, I will not repeat those actions. Leo has good skin that is healthy and soft. I know that the angels with help me to figure out what to do with the crones. Family should be easy, loving, and kind. You shouldn't hate speaking to them for fear that they will put negative labels on you. Maybe they will just leave me alone. Maybe they finally realize they aren't part of my life anymore which is why they didn't know I was pregnant. That should be a huge indicator that we really don't need to have a relationship. I need to attend to my son and myself. Leo is the symbol that they are no more, it is clear and direct so there can be no argument.

November 18, 2013

Today was a really good day for Leo and myself, we had a wonderful time playing and connecting. I was able to wear him in the carrier for a little this morning and he got into being worn. We would just stare into each other's eyes. He loves me so much that it is utterly overwhelming. He is completely in love with me. It is such a joyous feeling, this kind of complete love. He is an extension of me and in loving him so much I actually love myself in a healthy way that I am new to doing. We had a good day loving each other. This love is so easy and available; there is no fear as with other kinds of love. It feels so good to enjoy those kinds of moments for they are fully real and complete. He is such a good boy and so advanced for his age. He is just so wonderful and I feel so blessed that he came into my life.

January 1, 2014

Happy New Year! This is going to be a great year! I can't wait, it is finally here, for real! Everything is getting better and bringing me closer to my true self, my authentic self. I am actually really excited to see what happens and all the goodness that will come from the hard work I have done to bring myself to this point in my life. I feel calm and ready to begin my authentic life that is joyous and blissful. Leo is advancing so fast and he is such a wonderful baby. Joe and I are very grateful and happy to be parents to Leo. It is something that is very healing for Joe and myself. Joe has been a great dad, he always cares and always helps. He is really doing a great job as a dad!

January 30, 2014

So a few days ago my grandmother and then mother both called within a minute of each other. I have not talked to either one in a while, but I still ponder whether this is the right thing to do? Whenever I think of talking with either of them I go back to what hurtful things they have said to me in the past. When I was 18 and in the first semester of my freshman year in college my mother told me that my college education was a waste because I was going to die of AIDS anyway. Now for 15 years this memory was deeply buried in my subconscious. I literally had PTSD about having AIDS. One time in graduate school in a medical sociology class I broke down and started crying because a student was presenting about HIV. Even during my pregnancy I was terrified to get an AIDS test (even though I had 3 before) because these words lingered with me for so long. I wasn't even aware of it fully until I went through my major healing process when I was finishing my dissertation. After moving out from living with my ex Tom for about 2 years I almost immediately had the car accident where I flipped my car three times. Well the very next time I had sex after that I heard myself in my head saying I had AIDS all the time. I mean it was literally non-stop. It started the moment I woke up in the morning until I went to bed. I heard myself saying this in my head all day long and could not stop it. Even when I would speak to other people I would hear myself saying these things in my head. I didn't tell anyone about this for I was sure they would label me schizo or worse put me in an institution or something and of course I would never finish my Ph.D. I can't believe that I dealt with that for over a year. I was even worried that during my Ph.D. defense I wouldn't be able to concentrate because I would hear myself telling myself I had AIDS non-stop in my head. Thankfully after I moved in with Joe I told him what was happening and he didn't judge me or call me crazy or have me committed. Soon after it got much better and finally went away completely after my pregnancy blood work came back all healthy. Some days when I am lying in bed and all is calm I think back to that time and I really truly appreciate the peacefulness of the moment, that I don't have those intruding thoughts and how awful it was to not have control of my mind. I am really amazed I made it through that period.

The good part of that terrible experience is that it really pushed me into alternative healing. There was no way I would have ever told a doctor what was happening. With my mother being paranoid schizophrenic I am sure I would have gotten a similar label. Of all my challenges that was truly the hardest and most frightening because it was my mind and my mind had always been there for me in the past. When I think about it now I am sure that the accident in the car released my throat chakra (neck got whipped around) and it all came out (consciously) the next time I had sex since it triggered the PTSD into motion again. I was really scared and I remember thinking that I can't live like this, I can't hear myself saying these things in my head all day long, everyday with no end. In a way though I understand now that this was very important to my healing journey because I must have been saying these things to myself subconsciously for 15 years and only then did I really hear what I was saying to myself. From that torturous experience I became an energy healer and holistic healer so I understand why it had to happen. I never would take psych medication because that just prolongs the healing process. Honestly, I have never seen anyone heal while on psych meds. Of course I would self medicate but during this period I stopped smoking pot because it didn't even work anymore and I think it made me more anxious anyway.

I am really happy now to be fully present for my son. With him in my life I truly want to be the best version of myself. I started doing a mantra in my head during the day. I say "I love myself and I am beautiful." When I look in the mirror I really think I am starting to look different. Leo is such a positive influence on me. It makes me feel so good to be his mother, to feel like a normal person with a family and to feel like I am part of the greater cycle of life. I am really proud of myself for having a home birth and for breastfeeding. Just yesterday he started to bounce in his new jumperoo and it was so exciting to watch his new accomplishment. Being with him everyday makes me think a lot about my own childhood and I feel as though no one really loved me, really. I don't think anyone ever loved me the way that I love Leo. That makes me feel sad and somewhat victimized by my family but what is the point of dwelling on that now. I know that I am giving Leo everything I have, literally, he gets every part of me – physical, emotional, and spiritual. It may have been really rough at first, but things are much easier now that he is almost five months old. I feel really lucky to be able to be with him at home all day, however, it isn't really luck, I spent a great deal of time planning for things to be this way during that mental crisis period when I was finishing graduate school. I would literally lay in my bed and visualize myself in a glider rocking a baby. Seriously, I did this almost daily at night. I got all into the shamanic vision quest stuff at this time as well. I would go into this meditative state and I would talk with people – especially my professors in graduate school. I believe I really was talking with their spirits. Whatever reality I was tapping into was very real. I even saw things that were attached to people as well. There is a great deal that can be done in this other reality that I can go to, I am sure this is just the beginning.

February 1, 2014

Had a dream the other night that I was back in church. I was walking around looking at the daycare rooms for the children. This probably relates to how I am really focused on wanting to help children now, young children, not just the college kids that I used to teach. I basically saw them as children because most of what I taught was about emotion and trying to heal them for their own childhood family trauma. Now I think it would be easier to just go right to the children and not wait to heal them until college age. My classes were always more like group therapy because I had known that I wanted to help people and I originally wanted to be a therapist but then I realized that teaching would allow me to get to the people that weren't necessarily in therapy and to get to them at an age where major decisions had not already been made that were made without the healing of trauma and without a connection to their authentic self. I went ice skating last night by myself and it was wonderful, like being bathed in the energy of joy and happiness because it was all kids having a great time. I think I was the only adult there without a child. When Leo gets older we will definitely go ice skating, maybe he will even become an ice hokey player.

When I think of how I want to help children now I am so astounded at how deviant I became in my past, mostly my late 20s. I became very dark in a way, dark enough to have dated two drug dealers and a member of the mafia! I find it fascinating that at the time it was happening I didn't even mention these things in my diary for I could not even process that I was actually doing these things!

March 11, 2014

Had another dream two nights ago that I was in a church, actually walking through a church hallway with pews on the one side and then a table area on the other side. I walked through and then someone had said they liked the church that I was with so I offered to walk back and look again with them. When I looked again there were about eight children all sitting in a row at a table on the other side of the hallway across from the pews, their heads were down as if they were praying, they were young, around 5 or 6 years old. I wasn't sure if they liked being at the church or not because I couldn't see their eyes. This must be some kind of message about spirituality and children. Am I to help children through spirituality? I know that hallways indicate transition; I must be transitioning to this new phase with children. I will surely pay attention to anymore dreams I have and try to write them down as I had been doing for a while two summers ago. Dreams are very telling; they are the key to your true self. I read the other day that two alcoholic drinks at night result in removal of REM sleep, the kind of sleep in which one dreams. Wonder if that applies to all drugs and substances that affect consciousness? I probably cut myself off from my true self for a long time with substances, numbing everything I could in college and graduate school, I know that I wouldn't remember my dreams as well back then, maybe that was the point. My dreams scared me sometimes. I didn't want to know how far from myself I really was, it was just too much at that time. Now is the time, and I am ready for it all! I am sure I will be guided in what to do. I will listen, and pay attention to how everything feels, how my body reacts to different suggestions and guidance. My inner self will show me the way; I am wise and always have been, I just need to listen to my feelings.

August 31, 2014

Everything is so wonderful right now! I have been getting these NMT healings for myself and meditating regularly. My visualizations are working and Leo is becoming such a wonderful toddler. Leigh and I have even reconnected recently and have planned to hang out with our baby boys that are the same age. He will have his first birthday on Sept 6th and then we are going on our first family vacation to the shore. I have gotten back into my healing abilities and healed a friend of mine after a surgical procedure. She was shocked that she could feel the dark energy being removed off of her. Also, I have been thinking that I will activate my medium abilities as well. When I first saw that young boy who died in my old Philly apartment when I was 28 it frightened me a lot. Some women I saw on South Street explained to me that I can see spirits but that it scares me so I 'will' myself not to be able to see them. Maybe I should allow that ability to come through or at least be more open to being able to see into the spirit realm while I am awake. I think the key is relaxation and why it made spirit interaction more possible when I was asleep. When I do shamanic journeying I am awake, but very relaxed. Being relaxed (but without being medicated) is very important to connecting with the spirit realm and to manifestation. Now that I am older, I am more relaxed and I am able to just be with myself to allow these abilities to increase in power. Controlling my emotional reactions is extremely important. Now, when something happens that I do not want I remember to stop and tell myself 'what would you feel like if this were not happening, what would it feel like if you had all the things you want right now, and to hold onto those feelings as long as I can' as this is the path to having it all and to greatness!